35

Global Perspectives
China's Metamorphosis

PHOENIX TREE PUBLISHING INC.

Contents

Clothing

"Sweet, Your Smile Is as Sweet as Honey"	2
Colorful Cheongsams	6
I Like Chinese Kung Fu Robes	12
I Have the Same Set of Clothes as Jackie Chan	16
From "China's Li-Ning" to "the World's Li-Ning"	18

Food

Which Do You Prefer, Tea or Coffee?	22
Meat in a Vegetarian Restaurant	26
A Happy "Foodie"	30
The "Hottest" Chinese Woman	34
10 Years Eating in China	36

Living

Safety in Beijing	42
My Beijing Dream	44
Foreigners' Impressions of *Hutongs*	48
A Letter to Granny	52
Shanghai Memories	56

Travel

The Changes to Taxis in Beijing	62
A Walk through Yiwu to See the Changes	66
Slow and Fast: China Speed	70

Walking into a New Dawn on the First Rays of the Morning Sun	74
An Experience of the Spring Festival Travel Rush	78

Tourism

"If You Fail to Reach the Great Wall, Then You're Not a True Man"	84
The Imperial Palace: Growing Younger	88
Bridges—The Witnesses to Change	92
Searching for the Chinese Dream	94
The "Sought-After Quintessence" in the Greater Bay Area	96

Leisure

From Bruce Lee's Kung Fu Movies to *The Wandering Earth*	*100*
"Ambassador" Tchiegue's "Face-painted Life"	104
I Want to Star in the Spring Festival Gala	108
My Chinese Dream and Chinese Family	112
Yao Ming: China's Symbol Venturing in the NBA	116

Business

From a Sales Champion to an Entrepreneur	122
Smart Life in Beijing	126
"Made in China" and the Perceptions Thereof	130
The "Unseen and Untouched"	134
Shanghai—A City of Hope	136

Clothing

Clothing

"Sweet, Your Smile Is as Sweet as Honey"

Hwang Lanah (Republic of Korea)

"Sweet, your smile is as sweet as honey,

Just like flowers blooming in the breeze,

The sweet spring breeze…"

When I was young, my mom used to sing this Chinese song *Sweet as Honey*[1] and tell me this was one of the most popular songs in China that was also well liked in South Korea. Every time I heard the song, my lips would curl

---

1 *Sweet as Honey*, or *Tianmimi* in Chinese, is a well-known song performed by Teresa Teng.

into a smile and a "sweet" feeling would come over me. I couldn't wait to go to China one day and get close to this "sweet" country.

In 1999, when I was 12, I heard that Chinese young people really liked Korean fashion and called it "Korean influence" (韩流). At the same time, Hong Kong movies became popular in South Korea. The Hong Kong movie I remember most clearly was *Comrades: Almost a Love Story*. Accompanied by the familiar song of *Sweet as Honey*, the smile of Chinese actress Maggie Cheung touched my heart. From her undefiled beauty of 1986 to her gorgeous costume of 1997, Maggie Cheung's image had changed a lot, but to me, she would always remain sweet.

The scene where Li Qiao (Maggie) is sitting on the back of Li Xiaojun's (Leon Lai's) bike, with the wind gently blowing against her face and her beautiful sweet smile, will always remain in my heart. Her smiling face was the first Chinese woman's face I had seen and it was this face that strengthened my initial yearning for China.

In 2007, I came to China for the first time to study. Walking around the campus I could clearly see the youthfulness and vitality of the Chinese students. I realized the girls here didn't put much make-up on. Their plain faces had the typical pure sweet beauty of Chinese girls and were full of hope and expectation. We Korean girls would never walk around with plain faces. We longed for perfection in our looks and clothing, so our make-up was exquisite. On campus, we turned heads, and everyone could see from just a glance that we were Koreans.

Clothing

I remember in winter that year, I was in a dress waiting for a bus at the bus stop and a Chinese uncle looked at me curiously and asked, "Girl, are you not freezing?" He probably thought I was the most scantily clad person in all of Beijing that day!

I also remember one of my Chinese classmates telling me that only the Korean boys would wear their baseball caps in class, and he couldn't understand it. I explained to him that in South Korea, this was actually a kind of style and had nothing to do with practicality. The Chinese have a saying, "Clothes make the man." We Koreans also have a saying, "Clothes are a person's wings."

I returned to China in 2017 as a foreign teacher at my old university. I realized that "whether or not people wear caps, whether or not girls wear make-up on campus or how much people wear in winter" can no longer be used as the standard to differentiate between Chinese and Korean young people. My Chinese students told me that almost all of them had been abroad on holiday or as exchange students, because "Knowledge comes from books and experiencing the world." I observed that both their looks and clothes were confident and stylish, and their brilliant smiles had personality.

In 2019, I returned to China again and walked into my favorite university to do a PhD in Chinese studies. Seeing all the youthful faces and colorful clothes of the Chinese young people made me happy. The pure smile of Li Qiao (Maggie Cheung) in 1986, the confident smiles of the young women and the happy and fulfilled smiles of the women dancing in the square all appeared in my mind. What kind of China and what kind of Beijing is this? Chinese people and foreigners, Beijingers and outsiders, old-fashioned and modern people, with all their different lifestyles and faces, filled with hope for the future, are joined together, adding beauty to this modern capital. The beautiful song, *Sweet as Honey*, once again fills my mind:

"Where, where have I seen you before,

It's as if flowers are blooming in the spring breeze,

Ah, in my dream…

It was you, it was you,

It was you I saw in my dream…"

Clothing

Colorful Cheongsams

Clement Tanaka
(Indonesia)

Omurzakova Zhainagul
(Kirgizstan)

Irene Carmen Izarra
Sanz (Spain)

Janwiwattanakul
Pilaiwan (Thailand)

Le Thi My Ly (Vietnam)

Clement Tanaka (Indonesia)

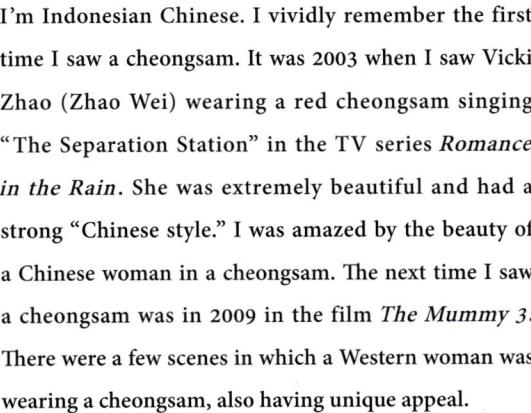

I'm Indonesian Chinese. I vividly remember the first time I saw a cheongsam. It was 2003 when I saw Vicki Zhao (Zhao Wei) wearing a red cheongsam singing "The Separation Station" in the TV series *Romance in the Rain*. She was extremely beautiful and had a strong "Chinese style." I was amazed by the beauty of a Chinese woman in a cheongsam. The next time I saw a cheongsam was in 2009 in the film *The Mummy 3*. There were a few scenes in which a Western woman was wearing a cheongsam, also having unique appeal.

When I came to China to study in 2015, encounters with the cheongsam became more frequent. From our teacher reading the story "The Eternal Snow Beauty" to the film *In the Mood for Love*, the subject cheongsam would always be mentioned. When the school organized an activity, many of the teachers or students would wear elegant cheongsams. There was a teacher in our college who really liked wearing them, so we gave her the nickname "Cheongsam Empress." In my mind, she almost wore a cheongsam all the time, in different colors and styles. Every time before class, we would guess which cheongsam she would be wearing that day.

Omurzakova Zhainagul (Kirgizstan)

I think that the cheongsam represents the beauty, elegance, and daintiness of Chinese women and because of its elegance, it has won favor across the world, becoming a source of inspiration for many designers. Global brands, such as Versace, Dior and Ralph Lauren, used elements of the cheongsam in their designs. These traditional elements have added more charm to modern clothing and it

proves the saying "National uniqueness leads to the path of global acceptance." Many foreigners like to try wearing a cheongsam after they come to China and I'm no exception. When I first came to China, I went to an exquisite cheongsam shop. The proprietress was wearing a cheongsam with a dark green velvet texture and a floral pattern embroidered in gold thread at the hem. With her hair fixed in a bun, she looked elegant and poised. I imagined myself looking that enchanting in a cheongsam, but unfortunately, when I tried a few on, they just didn't feel right. The proprietress said, "Cheongsams probably suit more mature women. Maybe come back and buy one in a few years." All my friends started laughing. Even though I wasn't able to buy one, I was still able to learn a lot about the cheongsam from the proprietress and I took lots of photos of beautiful cheongsams, so the trip was worthwhile.

Irene Carmen Izarra Sanz (Spain)

When I first came to China, at a carnival that the school organized, I saw a few Chinese girls wearing red cheongsams that were close-fitting, exquisite and sexy. They had done up their hair in a little, tight, round bun, with a beautiful hairpin holding it all together. At that time, I thought that the cheongsam was just a kind of costume for performances.

It was only later, after taking the Chinese culture class, where the teacher taught us about the cheongsam that I understood that is wasn't only for performing, but rather it is the traditional dress of Chinese women. Women in cheongsams are often seen on the streets. It suits the figures and temperament of Chinese women and really brings out the dignified elegance of oriental women, while also subtly hinting at the beauty of reticence, simplicity and exquisiteness.

Janwiwattanakul Pilaiwan (Thailand)

I still remember, when I was young, my family would sit down after dinner to watch a Chinese TV series. My favorite series was one about a Chinese emperor and his children. The main character was a very cute, lively and brave girl. To help her friend, the real princess, she pretended to be the princess and went into the palace. Many fun things happened. It was only after I came to China that I found out that series was called *My Fair Princess*.

In *My Fair Princess,* I like the princesses' clothes best. Their clothes were very unique. They were loose-fitting, the length was all the way down to the feet, the collar was high and round, the lines were straight and there were various colored patterns on them. The princesses wore a headdress, which I felt was very special. Some were big flowers and some were small, which I think was an indication of a princess's status. I was then a little girl and really wanted to wear these clothes, because I thought I would be like a princess if I did, but in Thailand there was nowhere to buy these clothes, so all I could do was to draw them on paper. It was only after I grew up and came to China that I realized they were actually women's outfits in the Qing Dynasty.

Speaking of the current cheongsams, I think they are also very beautiful. Every time I return to my motherland to spend a holiday, I bring one or two new cheongsams, which are either solid-colored or embroidered. After

hearing that I've come home, my best girlfriends will all eagerly come to my house and try on the cheongsams and enjoy our own fashion show.

Le Thi My Ly (Vietnam)

The cheongsam is an intelligent creation. I remember there was a Chinese teacher who told us that when she was abroad, she really liked wearing cheongsams, because she felt that they were like a name card for Chinese women. A woman wearing a cheongsam naturally emits an elegant, gentle temperament. After she returned to China, she noticed that more and more women there were also wearing cheongsams, but the beauty of the cheongsams was far from being fully revealed and was still waiting to be explored.

My teacher's words encouraged my interest in the cheongsam and I found out that there were many similarities between China's cheongsam and Vietnam's ao dai. They both cling to the body, making the body look tall and slender, revealing the beauty of oriental women's bodies. They also represent the Eastern understanding of the beauty of the human body. Maybe there is a certain amount of connection between cheongsam culture and ao dai culture.

▼ Colorful Cheongsams

Clothing

I Like Chinese Kung Fu Robes

Beishenaliev Azamat
(Kirgizstan)

I really like watching movies. Jackie Chan is one of my favorite actors and I'm sure other people like him too. If you randomly asked anyone on the streets of Kirgizstan what kind of shows they liked to watch as kids, the actors people talk about would almost always include the name Jackie Chan. If you followed up with the question of who their favorite funny kung fu actor is, or who the most famous Asian actor is, I can guarantee that the answer would be Jackie Chan. I think the answers would probably be the same, no matter which country you asked such questions in. Jackie Chan's kung fu movies are not

▼ I Like Chinese Kung Fu Robes

only loved by the Chinese, but have gained recognition and interest all over the world.

I watch the Oscars every year and still remember when, in 2016, Jackie Chan received an honorary Oscar. I wasn't surprised that he won an Oscar, I was more surprised by his clothes. I was puzzled at the time, why had Jackie Chan come on stage dressed like a nun? Luckily, at that time, I was taking a Chinese training program and was able to ask my teacher about it. The teacher burst out laughing when she heard my question. She explained that it wasn't a nun's outfit, but rather a traditional Chinese gown, also called a Chinese long gown.

It was the first time I'd heard of "long gowns" and I immediately looked up more information online. I found out that Jackie Chan actually liked wearing traditional Chinese long gowns for film festivals and award ceremonies, so it wasn't surprising that he had done the same for the Oscars. I think he hoped that through wearing these Chinese-style clothes he would be proclaiming to the world, "I am Chinese!"

Jackie Chan's movies not only allowed the world to see the uniqueness of Chinese kung fu, but also to see the charm of Chinese kung fu attire, because Jackie Chan often wears this traditional clothing as he shows off his amazing kung fu skills in the movies, especially in older movies like *Dragon Fist* and *New Fist of Fury*, etc. Jackie Chan's light and elegant kung fu costumes combined with his strong skills were unforgettable and from then on, my dream was to own a kung fu robe like Jackie Chan's.

The materials most used for making kung fu robes are silk and cotton. The

Clothing

robes are loose-fitting, to make it easier for martial artists to use their arms and legs. The smooth softness of silk and the plain softness of cotton help the robes to fit perfectly. It's almost as if the robes flow naturally into the shape of the kung fu movements, just like drifting clouds and flowing water.

In my fascination with Jackie Chan's movies, I often dreamt of being able to transform into a kung fu master after putting on the robe. After arriving in China for studies, I noticed there was an old kung fu master leading a group of people, with international students' faces among them, in white training robes on the square in front of the library. I joined the group of trainees and learned from the master, realizing one of my dreams. While practicing *taijiquan*, I also learned about the design elements of traditional Chinese clothes, like mandarin collars, buckles and a kind of Chinese jacket with buttons down the front. I also understood the importance of clothing color and how in Chinese culture different colors have different meanings. White, representing nature and peace, and black, representing mystery and wisdom, are the most common colors. Every morning, we would wear the same color when practicing. The lines were neat, movements were smooth and there was a sense of calmness enveloping everyone. As the rays of the morning sun illuminated us, I gradually started to experience the flexibility, toughness and harmony of the movements.

Thanks to Jackie Chan's patriotism and gift of acting, we have an opportunity to experience the uniqueness of Chinese kung fu. His perseverance and striving have made Chinese kung fu come alive. For many people, it was only after they came to know Jackie Chan that they started to take an interest in Chinese kung fu and learn about Chinese culture. I believe that the Jackie Chan who brought kung fu to the world will become a big part in the history of Chinese culture and globalization; while the kung fu costumes that are part of all this will emphasize the unique oriental connotations even more.

▼ I Like Chinese Kung Fu Robes

Clothing

I Have the Same Set of Clothes as Jackie Chan

Ahmed Magdy
Abdelhamed Elsayed
(David) (Egypt)

I'm an Egyptian who loves kung fu movies. I really want to meet my idol, Jackie Chan. He is famous in Egypt, in the whole of Africa and even in the whole world. The first time I saw Jackie Chan was in the movie *Drunken Master*. The movie has no exquisite backdrop or beautiful actors, but the aptly named drunken master, Jackie Chan, who was drunk but not drunk, attracted me. The image of him in his white shirt and blue training pants left an impression on me and I immediately decided to go to China some day. At that time, in my mind, China was a martial arts heaven with many heroes, where

▼ I Have the Same Set of Clothes as Jackie Chan

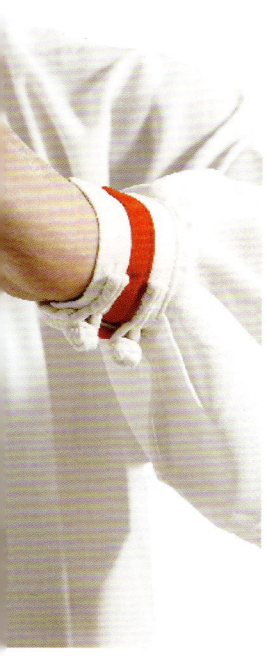

everyone liked to compete with each other and Jackie Chan was the best of them all. In order to get closer to my idol, I bought a white shirt and blue training pants and waited for the right occasion to show them off.

Not until I came to study in China did I notice that Chinese people nowadays didn't really wear that style of clothes any more. Everyone has their own fashion style, but sometimes there are still girls on the street wearing traditional Han Chinese costumes. Not all the people here practice kung fu. Later Jackie Chan was awarded an honorary Oscar. He deserved it. I still remember when Jackie Chan received his prize at the Oscars, he was wearing a long Chinese robe, embodying the Chinese style. In his acceptance speech he said, "I am very proud to be Chinese."

There are fans of Jackie Chan all over the world! As the most influential global Chinese star, Jackie Chan persists in wearing this style and wherever he goes, he never forgets to wear Chinese clothes. Jackie Chan is worthy of being called a descendant of the dragon and a spokesperson for China. We love Jackie Chan's movies, his enthusiasm, his Chinese style and his fashion sense.

After I came to China, I logged onto the online shopping center Tmall specially to buy a set of clothes the same as Jackie Chan's. Now, I already have two sets. One is the classic set from *Drunken Master* and the other is a set of his everyday style Chinese clothes.

What I would want most is to have a photo with him while wearing my white shirt mentioned before. Then I could tell my childhood self that "Your dream has come true!"

Clothing

From "China's Li-Ning" to "the World's Li-Ning"

Zach Mark Ireland
Splittgerber (USA)

I love sports. My favorite sport is basketball. When I have free time, I often play basketball with friends. I'm quite familiar with sports brands, among which China's Li-Ning is one of my favorites.

Its brand ambassador is Dwyane Wade, my favorite NBA basketball player. Every time Li-Ning comes out with a new Way of Wade limited edition, it's sold out straight away. Li-Ning's debut at the New York and Paris fashion weeks truly amazed me. The classic red and white, and the "tomato and egg stir-fry" colors were eye-catching. I really loved its brave yet retro color

From "China's Li-Ning" to "the World's Li-Ning"

ranges. The four characters 中国李宁 were proudly printed on the T-shirts, hoodies, jackets and handbags, which made a fan of Chinese characters like me fall in love at first sight. They even used the moment when Mr. Li Ning became an Olympic champion in the print design process, making it both retro and stylish. The name of the ACE range, 悟道, was really cool and reminded me of Lao Tzu's *Tao Te Ching*. It had a real Chinese style. 悟道2 ACE shoes are now very hard to buy. Many of my American friends even ask me to help them buy a pair.

A longstanding Chinese brand as it is, Li-Ning's road to success was not always plain sailing, and it experienced a long period of hardship. In 1989, after Li Ning, the king of gymnastics, retired, he created the brand Li-Ning and it reached its peak success in 2008, after Li Ning's appearance at the Olympics. But in 2011, because of an error in marketing strategy, Li-Ning experienced a fall from success to hardship, and from 2012 to 2014 the company was stuck in a quagmire of huge losses. In order to revive the company, the founder Li Ning personally embarked on a series of drastic reforms. It was only in 2018, when the brand appeared at the New York fashion week, that it was able to turn everything around. In those years, the brand used its own actions to prove its own slogan: "Anything is possible."

Besides Li-Ning, other Chinese brands such as Anta and Warrior are also internationally popular. I see more and more Chinese businesses going global. I hope that more companies can be like Li-Ning, using their own understan-ding of the brand to innovate continuously and create their own destinies.

Food

Food

Which Do You Prefer, Tea or Coffee?

Maria Camila Xiaosi
Rincon (Canada)

My mom is from Chengdu, China, and I was born in Canada. I went to my mom's hometown over the holidays and grew fond of drinking tea. As soon as I got to my Granny's house, she offered me a cup of hot tea, and I was moved. I tried many different kinds of tea, such as red tea, black tea, jasmine tea, and I really liked all of them. There's a saying in Chengdu, "Sunny days are few, but tea rooms are many." A bowl of tea, a table of Mahjong, a group of friends and a relaxed chat is a common scene on the streets of Chengdu. It's so nice! There are all kinds of tea shops, tea rooms and tea houses providing places

where the bustling and busy people of today can catch a moment of peace. I really like Chengdu and enjoy the lifestyle of the people there.

My dad is from Colombia, a place that produces quality coffee, so drinking coffee is a part of daily life. Now there are also a lot of Chinese young people who drink coffee and there are a lot of coffee shops. I've been to a few and found the coffee there is very good. Also, when I was traveling in Yunnan, I discovered something new: Pu'er City in Yunnan not only grows tea trees, but also coffee plants! Many global coffee brands have established bases there for planting coffee.

China is a country where tea culture is advocated and people love drinking tea. All my Chinese friends, whether in Beijing or in Shanghai, have tea sets in their homes and keep the tradition of tea drinking. Once, in Vancouver, I took part in a tea art class. It was

organized by a Chinese and attracted many people who were interested in tea ceremonies. I think that tea is a symbol of Chinese culture. No matter where a Chinese person is, they will always offer tea when hosting people. No matter how fast China develops, every Chinese family will keep the tradition of making tea.

As the saying goes, "Western coffee and Chinese tea." Exchanges among countries are more and more frequent. Coffee and tea have also spread to different countries and have gradually merged due to exchanges.

When my dad came to China in 1992 to study Chinese medicine, there were not many coffee shops in China at that time and very few varieties of coffee. Compared to China back then, now there are a lot of coffee shops and you can find coffee brands from all over the world. People can choose whether to drink coffee or tea according to their own tastes. What's interesting is that Chinese young people have slowly started to like coffee, while my dad and I have started to like drinking tea.

▼ Which Do You Prefer, Tea or Coffee?

Meat in a Vegetarian Restaurant

Siriwachirakun Songpon
(Lin Yaonan) (Thailand)

I'm a person who has never liked eating vegetables. Even if I ate a little bit, I would spit it out straight away. To me, vegetables are horrible, bitter and disgusting. I feel bad as soon as I take a bite. My family and friends all encouraged me to eat more vegetables and less meat, because even though vegetables are disgusting to me, they are full of nourishment. But in the end, I still couldn't eat them. Later, someone told me that Chinese chefs could make vegetables taste like meat. How was this possible? Vegetables and meat clearly taste different! When I was in Thailand, I already knew that Chinese

▼ Meat in a Vegetarian Restaurant

people really pay attention to their food. The food is not only rich in variety, but the color, smell and taste are also perfect. But, for a person who has hated vegetables since childhood, how would I not be able to tell whether I was eating meat or vegetables?

One day, my parents and I went on holiday to Hainan and the tour guide took us to worship the Bodhisattva Guanyin of the South China Sea. In that temple there was a famous vegetarian restaurant that our tour guide said made very good food. He said that even though everything was made with vegetables, when you actually ate it, it tasted like meat. If you closed your eyes, it would be impossible to tell that you were actually eating vegetables. I couldn't wait to try the food and see if what I had heard before was real!

When the first dish was served, I thought, "Is this not just braised beef? Regardless of how I looked at it, it looked like meat, but our guide assured me that this really was made with vegetables. I still found it hard to believe and the only way to really know was to taste it. But when I took a bite, it still tasted like meat. From the color, smell and taste, it was just like braised beef. The tour guide explained that this dish was actually made of konjac, because the texture of konjac is similar to that of meat. The chefs had to go through a complicated process in order to finally complete this kind of "braised beef."

Unbelievable! The second dish was braised meatballs in brown sauce that was actually made from dried bean curd, white gourd and flour. The third dish was vegetarian chicken, which was made from thin sheets of dried bean curd. The tour guide said that this dish was a result of combining Buddhist culture and food culture, and the cooking technique had a long history. I really admired the chefs of the vegetarian restaurant for actually being able to make vegetarian dishes that tasted like different kinds of meat. It really opened my eyes and I was able to have a great meal!

From then on, I've realized that vegetables can also taste good. The vegetarian restaurants show the concept of having a natural, healthy lifestyle and also the supreme skillfulness of Chinese chefs. Although vegetarian dishes are more expensive than normal ones, it doesn't mean that the cost of vegetables is more expensive, but rather that the cooking techniques are more complicated than for normal food. What a great invention! It allows a person like me who doesn't eat vegetables to actually start to like eating veggies. This means that my family and friends won't have to worry about my health any more.

I had long heard about China's extensive knowledge and long-established history of culinary expertise, and once I had been to the vegetarian restaurant, I was able to experience that more deeply for myself. In ancient China, people could rely on their intelligence to come up with many different cooking methods. Whilst nowadays, Chinese people have not only continued using those ancient cooking methods, but have also built on the original culinary foundation, making even more, tastier, and healthier Chinese food. I think this is probably also the reason why Chinese food is loved by people all over the world! The Chinese stress that "food is the primary need of the people" and each dish reflects the Chinese people's collective strength and intelligence. I think that foreign students that come to China to study can learn about the history and culture whilst trying Chinese food and tasting the mythical origin of every delicacy.

▼ Meat in a Vegetarian Restaurant

A Happy "Foodie"

Vusal Guliyev
(Azerbaijan)

Although I'm from Azerbaijan, I was born and grew up in Kazakhstan. When I was young, my parents brought me to Russia, Turkmenistan, Ukraine, Georgia, Turkey and a lot of other places, and wherever we went, I would always try the local delicacies. The mystery of Chinese food is beyond anyone's imagination. I became a happy "foodie."

I still remember going out for dinner with some friends after I had just arrived in China. When we got to a restaurant, the waiter recommended that we order "volcanic snow", which is actually just another name for tomato

slices with sugar, but the name volcanic snow is more artistic; "peerless double peppers" is just red chili peppers fried with green chili peppers…

Compared with in other countries, the time spent sitting at the dinner table in China was the most interesting.

To tell you the truth, I'm not too keen on eating, but I love Chinese food. Big plate chicken, pita bread soaked in lamb soup, Shaanxi cold rice noodles, cayenne pepper beef… Too many to count and too many to name. The more you eat, the tastier it gets; the tastier it gets, the more you want to eat. The most peculiar thing is that in China, no matter what I eat, I don't grow fat, but as soon as I go back to Azerbaijan for the holidays and even though I'm especially careful, my weight still starts to go up! Why is this? After much thought, I still couldn't get my head around it, but later decided that it was probably to do with drinking tea before and after a meal in China. In many restaurants, before they serve the food, they serve a pot of tea. Tea culture is a part of Chinese food culture. Maybe the Chinese secret to health is drinking tea.

I have never seen a country that places more importance on eating than China. The way Chinese people greet each other is also different from foreigners. English speakers say "How are you?" or "Good morning!",

Food

whereas the first thing the Chinese say on seeing each other is "Have you eaten?" This is because for Chinese people, "eating" is a culture of its own and this is visible from their language, lifestyle, history and culture. Chinese people really do believe that "food is the primary need of the people." In China, any situation can be described with "eating." For example, being jealous is described as "eating vinegar"; being accused by someone else is called "eating a lawsuit"; suffering a loss is called "eating a loss"; if you can't stand something, you say "eating something you could not digest"; being popular is "eating well," etc.

No matter whether they are discussing business, making friends, or just meeting with others, Chinese people will always share food together. Other than the dishes themselves, Chinese people's joy in sharing may be an underlying reason why Chinese food is so loved all around the world.

▼ A Happy "Foodie"

The "Hottest" Chinese Woman

Shyshov Iegor (Ukraine)

The Chinese "Lao Gan Ma" (literally "Old Godmother") is the best chili paste I've ever tasted. I often see my wife, who is Chinese, taking a spoonful of red paste out of a glass jar. I tried it once out of curiosity. It was like opening a window to a new world. It's not like the Mexican Havana chili paste that burns your mouth off, but the taste is pleasant. You can feel the fragrantly crisp taste of the chili balancing on the edge of your tongue. "Lao Gan Ma" is a mixture of fried chilies, garlic, onions mixed with peanuts and soybeans that creates an incomparable texture with multiple levels of taste that stimulates your taste buds.

I've seen many foreigners online who have used "Lao Gan Ma" to create foods that are a mixture of both Chinese and Western foods. For example, "Lao Gan Ma" vanilla cheese, "Lao Gan Ma" toast and some even made "Lao Gan Ma" desserts by putting a spoonful of red "Lao Gan Ma" on their ice cream… It's really eye-opening!

On Facebook, they have a designated page for "Lao Gan Ma" fans. All the "Lao Gan Ma" fans around the world are gathered here and the most popular topic of their discussions is from which Chinese supermarkets they can buy authentic "Lao Gan Ma." "Lao Gan Ma" is even sold on Gilt, a website for buying discounted luxury items. So if you can afford "Lao Gan Ma," then you're pretty well off. Even though the price of "Lao Gan Ma" abroad is not cheap, it does not stop us from happily buying it, because we are real fans of "Lao Gan Ma."

"Lao Gan Ma" was even at the New York fashion week. Many of the different brands printed the "Lao Gan Ma" logo on their clothes! It was really cool!

My Chinese teacher told me the story of Tao Huabi, the founder of "Lao Gan Ma." I really respect the way she kept her feet on the ground, strived to improve, and her integrity. This must be the "spirit of craftsmanship" of Chinese people.

Famous Chinese snacks like "Little Racoon" instant noodles have also become very popular abroad. Every time I go back to my home country, I always bring some for my friends.

There are so many delicious Chinese foods that one can hardly try them all. I hope that Chinese food can continue to develop and become as popular as "Lao Gan Ma," allowing the world to taste more.

Food

10 Years Eating in China

Sabrina Krebs (USA)

The first time I visited Beijing was when I was only eight years old. It was in January of 2008, and I remember gazing at all the Chinese New Year decorations when passing by the restaurants as I wandered down the winding streets.

That year had an especially cold and dry winter. Despite the weather, I remember the warmth and energy I felt when we went to the temple fairs. I remember going to the temple fairs for the first time, and with the congregations of people, the popping of firecrackers and celebrational

drumming, the red glow of lanterns and of course, the good smell coming off the freshly made *bingtanghulu*, I felt warm down to my toes.

Bingtanghulu is a favorite street food made by stringing Chinese hawthorns on a skewer, then dipping and coating it in melted sugar, which then dries and hardens into a delicious treat for children at that time of year. And much like the treat itself, Beijing was sweet, upon our arrival—but I soon discovered its complex layers and depth concealed beneath the surface.

At that time, I went to school on Laiguangying East Road, and this street was packed with some of the best food stalls and restaurants. I remember a sit-down family restaurant with large circular tables serving family dishes, with smells of oil wafting through the air as we were served fried mandarin fish. Further down the street, there was a small restaurant that served the most delicious *chaobing*, a stir-fried dish with chopped-up pancakes. Across from it, I remember the breakfast stall I'd visit for northern-style *xiaolongbao* (soup dumplings), soymilk, *youtiao* (fried donut sticks) and *doufunao* (soft bean curd). Old neighbors stopping by to chat and people running in and out to grab food before they started their days gave this area a wonderful sense of community.

Food

As the next few years went by and the community area was rebuilt and developed, the surrounding little restaurants were either renovated or replaced one after another. One day, I discovered that my favorite dumpling restaurant had also closed down. At the time, I was very disappointed, because that restaurant's dumplings were special; all were made fresh from scratch, and the outer skin was nice and thin with a delicious al dente bite. And they had the most delicious fillings, my favorite being the beef and fennel. After much searching, my family and I eventually found another local dumpling restaurant around the renovated community that replaced our old favorite and became the new family dumpling spot.

Another few years passed, bringing on another round of renovations. With it, a new Halal grilled skewers place opened as well as a new *jianbing* (a fried crepe with egg, onions, and other toppings) stand. This place's *jianbing* had a crunchier, crispier crepe in the Shandong style, which was harder to find compared with its softer, more common style of preparation. The vendor also made their own home-made plum sauce and had fresh greens from the market on hand every morning. Much like how the nation itself was evolving, so were the restaurants, and shops. Paying with cash was no longer the only option; I could also scan a QR code to pay. When I first moved to Beijing, I never imagined how dramatically and quickly the city would change over those few years, and the mobile wallet transaction system is just one of the many ways in which everyday routines have changed.

Fast forward to the end of my last full year in Beijing, May 2016, to my high-school graduation ceremony. The ceremony, held in the Confucian Temple, was in the quintessential spot: a perfect mix of honoring traditional Confucian scholar ceremonies while embracing them in the 21st century. As we left the temple to go home, I still remember eating *aiwowo* (a steamed cake with sticky-rice filling) and *lüdagun* (a pastry made of steamed glutinous millet flour) as we walked back; thinking back on it, I can still taste the sweetness in my mouth, hear the laughter of my friends filling the street, and the warmth of that summer sun.

Leaving a city that I had lived for ten years was tough. But, now as a student majoring in nutrition and living near Manhattan's Chinatown—a hub of cuisine from all over China, I have a deeper appreciation of what was so readily available and accessible to me growing up. No culture's food has had the breadth and depth to what China has, nor the globally widespread dissemination that we have seen.

If China's growth could be boiled down to one thing, for me, it would be best represented by the changes I observed and the food experiences I enjoyed on that small section of Laiguangying East Road. The same could be said of my childhood living as an American expat in China—as China changed, those changes rippled through the community around me, and I changed and grew as well. I'm thankful for the experiences I have had, learning through living in a community anchored in the shared enjoyment of food.

Living

Safety in Beijing

Thais Macedo de Oliveira (Brazil)

Ana Paula da Costa Torres (Brazil)

In Chinese, the character 安 originally meant a virtuous woman in a house. While, for us Brazilian girls, whether or not a girl can go out alone is the standard by which we measure the safety in a country or city.

After we had arrived in Beijing, we kept up our vigilance at first. Every time I went out with my dad, I'd bury my phone deep in my handbag. But in the streets and alleys, we saw many Chinese girls walking around by themselves, holding their phones in their hands even on the crowded buses and metro. We gradually started to realize that Beijing was a safe place.

▼ Safety in Beijing

During the year of study in Beijing, we really enjoyed the freedom and sense of safety. As we got to know China better, we found that the people's sense of safety came from the traditional Chinese cultural ideology of prizing "harmony," from the successful implementation of laws and regulations by the government.

The Chinese police are very strict and when something happens, they act immediately. Because of this, people have confidence in the law and understand the consequences of breaking it. We really enjoy this free and safe environment, but we know that this high-quality life is hard to come by. I've heard my Chinese friends say, "There is no such thing as a peaceful life without someone who bears the burden for you." The longer we live here, the more we understand this sentence. Behind the peaceful life lie the powerful policies of the Chinese government and the effective implementation of them by the police.

It is because of the safety in Beijing that we don't have to stay at home and be a quiet woman. We can go out on our own, no matter day or night. We can choose to use whatever form of public transport we want, whether it's the metro or a shared bike. We are grateful for Beijing's safety, which allows us to become women who can leave the house with confidence.

Living

My Beijing Dream

Mounoukou Herica
(Republic of the Congo)

In 2013, I was 20 years old. I met a Chinese friend whose warmth and kindness made me hope to learn about this far-off, mysterious country. I had a dream that one day, under the blue sky of Beijing, I would experience the atmosphere of this far-off country.

In order to understand China and realize my Beijing dream, I started learning Chinese in the Confucius Institute at Marien Ngouabi University.

My Beijing Dream

We nicknamed it the "En (恩)[1] Confucius Institute" in order to thank the Confucius Institute for its kindness. "*Ping ping ze ze ping ping ze*, how clever the Chinese are and how beautiful the Chinese language is…"[2] Even though Chinese was a bit difficult, I was confident that I could learn it. I also often listened to Chinese songs.

My Beijing dream was realized in 2016. In Beijing, I went to many places of interest like the Great Wall, the Imperial Palace, Tian'anmen Square, Beijing National Stadium (Bird's Nest), Beijing National Aquatics Centre (Water Cube), and even saw the new headquarters of CCTV (China Central Television). These places made me realize that Beijing is a city of history and modernity, including the world's greatest Great Wall and the world's most modern buildings.

I saw something very special in Beijing. Every morning, elderly people would all gather to practice *taijiquan* and every evening, old ladies would gather to do square dancing. It was great! On weekend mornings, I would join the throng of elderly people practicing *taijiquan* and they would tell me that if I continued to practice, I would strengthen my body and mind. I enjoyed the

---

1 "En (恩)" in Chinese means "grace" or "kindness," but is also the first character in the Chinese name of the Marien Ngouabi University (恩古瓦比大学).
2 This is an excerpt from a Chinese song about the Chinese language. The first line (*in italics*) describes the tone pattern of the Chinese language.

square dancing even more. Every time I saw the old people dancing in the evening, I would join in and start dancing, just like in Congo when everybody danced together. I think that Chinese old people are really cute!

I am a very forgetful girl, but in Beijing, I got back what I'd lost more than once. Every time there was an emergency, Chinese people were always willing to help. One day, I went to collect a package and when I got back, I realized I had lost my phone, so I immediately used my roommate's phone to dial my number. A warm voice answered from the other end in the local Beijing dialect and said, "Ah, so you remembered your phone! I'll wait for you to come and get it!" Another time, I fell asleep on a bus and my phone slid to the floor. A lady woke me up and said, "Hey! Young lady, you dropped your phone! Be more careful and watch that you don't miss your stop!" Living in Beijing, I've felt how the people in Beijing care about each other. The people of Beijing are very honest and trustworthy.

I have experienced the tradition and modernity of Beijing. It is developing every minute and every second of every day. As a foreigner, my deepest impression is that Beijing has been attracting young people from all over the world.

I hope I can become an envoy of cultural exchanges between China and Congo one day and tell the stories during my stay in Beijing, bringing with me the friendliness, affability and kind-heartedness of the people of Beijing.

▼ My Beijing Dream

Living

Foreigners' Impressions of *Hutongs*

Siriwachirakun Songpon
(Lin Yaonan) (Thailand)

Ka Kyosei (Japan)

Ahmed Magdy
Abdelhamed Elsayed
(David) (Egypt)

Temur Malik (Tajikistan)

▼ Foreigners' Impressions of *Hutongs*

Lin Yaonan: Hi, guys, I'm happy to see you all again in Beijing!

David: Hey, Yaonan, I heard that this time you returned as a representative of one of the most famous schools in Bangkok, Sansheng Middle School?

Temur: Yaonan is Head of the Chinese language program at Sansheng Middle School.

Lin Yaonan: Yes, this time I brought my students to Beijing on a study tour. Our school thought that students would be able to experience the thousands of years of history in Beijing and be able to commune with ancient philosophers of Chinese civilization. They could also experience different cultures of the world and embrace what's new in technology and the humanities.

David: Yeah, Beijing is full of new surprises every second and every minute of every day.

Temur: I like old Beijing's *hutongs* (alleys), especially in the Houhai area, where music lovers from all over the world gather and new stories happen every day. All the different local snacks are on sale there too. Everything about Houhai and the surrounding lanes and alleys has an intimate feel to it.

Ka Kyosei: If you walk into an alley, it is highly probable that at the

Living

entrance, you will see the former residence of some historical figure. These are the alleys of Beijing; every brick and every tile has its own history, full of things you couldn't imagine.

David: This is a city of stories. I like to walk through the alleys around Nanluoguxiang. Every courtyard there seems to have been lived in by some famous person, and has a hidden history. For example, the former residence of Wanrong[1] before she got married is in one of the alleys off Nanluoguxiang. You would never guess if you didn't look carefully and observe the four characters 婉容故居 (Wanrong's Former Residence) on the door. There are also many nobles' houses in the area, with signs saying "cultural relic" on the gray-brick, gray-tile gates. It's not far away from the Forbidden City and the Chinese would say it is a treasure land.

Ka Kyosei: Some residences from the Ming and Qing dynasties have changed owners in modern times, such as Lin Haiyin's former residence, which during the Qing Dynasty used to be the Jinjiang Guildhall. I, like Lin

---

1 Wanrong is the last empress of the Qing Dynasty (1616-1911).

▼ Foreigners' Impressions of *Hutongs*

Haiyin, was born in Tokyo, but study and live in Beijing. In her book *My Memories of Old Beijing*, she describes life in Beijing as being like life in "a golden age, reflected in the glazed tiles of the Forbidden City," and I agree. I went there last week and noticed that the three old Chinese scholar trees, with their lush branches reaching to the sky, were still there just as Lin Haiyin described them. Walking down the alley in front of the residence, I imagined experiencing the Beijing of ninety years ago portrayed in *My Memories of Old Beijing* along with Yingzi[1], bustling and lively, with long alleys, thick shade of trees, and a strong accent of Beijing dialect…

Lin Yaonan: Hearing what you said, I think it was sensible for us to come to Beijing on this study tour. In addition to historical relics such as the *hutongs*, the Forbidden City, the Temple of Heaven and the Great Wall, I may also take my students to experience modern Beijing and its metro, shared bikes, flyovers and Central Business District. Historical humanity and modern technology are interwoven and merge in this international metropolis. The students can experience a three-dimensional, authentic and diverse Beijing! For our first stop this weekend, I'll take them to Nanluoguxiang!

---

1 Yingzi is the main character in *My Memories of Old Beijing*.

Living

A Letter to Granny

Kim Cherry (Republic of Korea)

April 05, 2019

Dear Granny,

How are you doing in heaven?

Did you know that I really miss you? It's been nine years. I always see your smiling face, almost as if you've never left.

Do you still remember what I look like, Granny? I'm much thinner than I used to be, and taller too. I still remember you told me that China was an

A Letter to Granny

ancient, mystical country. I came to China thinking of you and spent the autumn, winter and spring in Beijing.

Autumn in Beijing is like the drawings that my brother and I drew when we were young. My brother's drawings were full of colors, just like the autumn leaves in Beijing. Clumps, clusters and piles of fiery red maple leaves, yellowish-green gingko leaves and golden poplar leaves are like intimate friends whispering secrets to each other, making it feel as if you're in wonderland. Xiangshan (Fragrant Hill) Park is the best place to go and enjoy the red leaves. I want to go for a walk with you among the colorful sea of leaves on Fragrant Hill and listen to the rustling sound.

Winter in Beijing is like mornings in our house. When I was a kid, I was scared of the long night and would often run to Granny's room and ask if I could sleep in your bed. I felt safe and secure with Granny. The winter nights in Beijing were also very long, cold, dark, and I felt scared and lonely. I was fortunate to have met a lot of warm-hearted Chinese friends. They gave me warmth and helped me to get through my fear of dark nights. When I was sick, they would take me to the hospital. When I had difficulties with my studies, they would tutor me. When I lacked self-confidence, they would encourage me. When I was homesick, they would stay with me and make small talk. All these things made me feel the warmth of spring in the cold of the winter in Beijing. Granny, please remember them and keep them safe, because to me there are no better friends than them!

"The rain is incessant on Qingming Day, and men and women walk sadly on the way." Today is the Chinese Qingming Festival. Everybody has three days off when they commemorate their ancestors by sweeping their tombs and offering sacrifices. Granny, if there is an afterlife, I want to take you with me into the autumn, winter and spring of Beijing.

Spring in Beijing is just like dad, great at growing flowers! Do you still remember the year when you brought a pot of orchids to our house? That pot of plants was a bit withered, but under my dad's care, it grew more and more beautiful by the day! There is a line in a poem about spring in Beijing that says, "As though a gust of spring wind swept by overnight, bringing thousands upon thousands of pear trees into bloom." During the spring in Beijing, all the plants are full of life. Peach blossoms, winter jasmines, apricot flowers, pear blossoms and cherry blossoms all vie with each other for attention, causing people to linger. If you want to see the cherry blossoms, Granny, then I would take you to Yuyuantan Park. The cherry blossoms of Yuyuantan Park are known to almost every household and there is a cherry blossom festival every year. It's amazing! I want to sit with you beside the pond and feel the beauty and peace of the "moonlight illuminating the pear blossoms."

Zhuangzi said, "Life is short and goes by quickly." I lived less than a year in Beijing. Although it was a short time, I still made some great memories. Granny, was it you who watched over me and kept me safe every day from heaven? I think that it definitely was you taking care of me. It's almost as if I was held in your embrace every day. I still remember your face and voice, and remember how you would always say to me, "You, dear, are my pride and joy!" It's only because of these words that I keep striving and I will always make you proud of me!

I wish you all the best in heaven!

Your loving granddaughter,

Cherry

▼ A Letter to Granny

Living

Shanghai Memories

Iruoma Ekpunobi (USA)

In 2009, my family found out that we would be moving from the quiet Chapel Hill, North Carolina, USA to the bustling Shanghai, China. My parents—Nigerian immigrants who understood how much of a cultural shock the move would be for my brother and I—signed us up for weekly "Chinese cultural classes," in which a nice lady named Veronica taught us the dos and don'ts of living in China. My brother, Ik, and I learned the meaning of the number 4, how to use chopsticks, and some amazing facts about China and its people that were so fascinating that it was hard to believe they were true.

▼ Shanghai Memories

Despite the "cultural classes," many things in China would still feel unbelievable a year later, by which time our family had physically relocated to Shanghai. One of the first things that I found most astonishing was that hundreds of millions of people would leave the cities where they work and return to their hometowns for the Chinese New Year every year. This annual movement of people constitutes the largest human migration in the entire world. This worldwide record is occurring annually in China, and I hadn't known anything about it before moving to the country.

I quickly realized that China was nothing like what I thought it would be, and it was nothing like most Americans pictured or could even imagine.

My father, being an architect who loves city planning, would often take me to the Shanghai Urban Planning Exhibition Hall, where I would see incredibly detailed scaled models of the city, and admire how everything was neatly divided into city blocks.

Shanghai is a very big city in terms of landmass, and with such a large population, it leans on its developed and convenient transportation system to move people around quickly and reliably. Shanghai has an intricate network of highways and expressways that cross over each other like a multi-layered concrete web.

Shanghai is split into two halves, Pudong and Puxi[1], which residents can commute between using any of the many bridges and tunnels connecting one side to the other. Shanghai also boasts an efficient, inexpensive, and clean metro system which my friends and I took on most weekends from the residential Pudong area we lived in, to enjoy the nightlife of Puxi. During that period of living in Shanghai, it seemed everything around me was constantly improving. There was never a day I went outside and didn't see some new construction projects, some of which could be completed in only a couple of months. Right now, Shanghai is a very young and exciting city, and as such, is continuously attracting young and vigorous people. But, it also values its rich history, and the city government works diligently to preserve the "Old City" buildings.

Out of all the amazing opportunities that living in Shanghai gave me, I am most grateful for the opportunity to have been exposed to and immersed in a Chinese language environment. Many expat families look for a *baomu*, or domestic helper, who speaks English, but my mother insisted on finding someone who would only speak to me and my brother in Chinese. This allowed us to keep practicing our Mandarin Chinese outside of school, where we already took Mandarin classes every day. If a student's learning comes only from a textbook, his or her knowledge is limited to the scope of the chapters, whereas in my case, most of the Chinese vocabulary I've grasped has been picked up from various interactions in life. Besides this, I also got to study some of the Shanghai dialect in addition to Mandarin. My immersion in the Chinese language also made it easier to pick up on certain aspects of Chinese culture that were new to me. One such concept was "saving face," or protecting someone else's dignity and preserving your humility in social

---

[1] Pudong and Puxi literally translate as "east of the Huangpu River" and "west of the Huangpu River."

situations, with them protecting your dignity in return. I also learned many other small cultural norms, such as handling/receiving business cards or any important document with both hands, to show attention and care.

Living in Shanghai was an experience full of lessons for me, and I felt that in those five years I only scratched the surface of the wonders China holds. I would suggest everyone to visit China. It would be a life-changing experience in a country like no other.

Travel

Travel

The Changes to Taxis in Beijing

Kunimoto Nobue (Japan)

In Beijing, taking a taxi is a joyful experience, like taking a scenic drive around Beijing. For us foreigners, chatting with the taxi drivers is a good chance to get to know this historical city. I once met a driver who had been driving taxis for over 30 years, who told me a story of years gone by. During the 1980s in Beijing, driving a taxi was as cool as flying a plane nowadays and all the kids in the *hutongs* (narrow lanes) would stare in awe and curiosity… As I chatted to the driver, I was transported back in time to the roads of Beijing when I was a child.

The Changes to Taxis in Beijing

Because of my parents' work, I was very young when I came to Beijing. Other than "Crown Comfort" taxis, the yellow *miandi* also left an impression on me. *Miandi* was a kind of minivan taxi that became popular in the 1990s. The whole van from the body to roof light was all yellow, so people gave it the nickname "yellow bug." The price of taking a "yellow bug" was very cheap and the large body meant that it had a large capacity, which made it perfect for transporting people or things, but the seats were very hard, so sitting inside wasn't a comfortable experience. It also felt like a bumpy ride. These taxis didn't have any air conditioning either, so other than being cheap, you couldn't really say it was comfortable. In spite of all this, at that time, the "posh yellow bugs" quickly became a popular mode of transport for the people of Beijing.

Later, the "yellow bug" got a new friend called "Xiali." This was a type of car that had a fully red body that was small like a red ladybird. In my childhood memories, Beijing was full of these red and yellow cabs.

Slowly, more types of cars like Citroën Fukang and VW Jetta appeared, each differing in price. Different car models met the differing needs of people.

Other than the colors yellow and red, there was another color that left an impression on me, blue. In the 1990s, there were also a lot of tricycles, which were different to the electric tricycles that you can see today, because you had to pedal them with your feet. There was a blue and white awning which could be collapsed to catch some sun during nice weather and put up to block the wind and rain in bad weather. Sitting in the back, you could feel the rhythm

Travel

of the driver pedaling and the gentle speed allowed you to take in the sights of Beijing's lanes and alleys. There were also small buses that you could take, fitting around ten people. These could be stopped anywhere along the road and didn't have any set bus stops. There was also a type of motorbike taxi that had to be started by pulling a rope, causing a puff of black smoke to burst out of the exhaust, thus the nickname *yiliuyan* (a streak of smoke).

As China's economy developed and the road traffic was standardized, these taxicabs of every description disappeared from history's stage. If I'm not mistaken, the yellow minivans were "laid off" in 1999, the red Xiali "retired" in 2006, and the rest of the cabs also "vanished from the face of the earth."

Replacing them are the taxis "wearing motley attire" of red and yellow or yellow and green, that are very comfortable. In the wake of the continuous development of automotive energy, cars have appeared that are not just powered by petrol, such as petrol and electric hybrids and purely electrical cars, etc. The roads are wider, traffic is more standardized, and streets are more beautiful.

As people start to pay more attention to environmental protection, more people are choosing to use greener modes of transport like the metro, buses or shared bicycles. People are more conscious of being environment-friendly, which can only be good.

These years, taxis have changed immeasurably, but what has never changed is the warm-heartedness of the people in Beijing and Beijing's taxi drivers, and my interest in chatting with them. Taxi drivers are still the same as they were years ago, easy to listen to as they cordially tell stories of Beijing in their local, earthy Beijing drawl.

▼ The Changes to Taxis in Beijing

A Walk through Yiwu to See the Changes

Park Jongyeon (Republic of Korea)

In 1986, almost everybody around me thought: "In the future, China will become one of the world's economic powers and the prospects for Chinese majors will be very good...," so I chose Chinese as my major. There is a saying in China, "Choose what you love, and love what you choose." Since the first day of my enrollment, I have always been fully interested in Chinese and loved the course. Now, my students are different. Many of them are hazy and confused about their future. They don't know what they want to do after they graduate, and they don't even know why they picked Chinese as their major.

▼ A Walk through Yiwu to See the Changes

As their teacher, it is my job to help them understand the value of their major and my responsibility to help them realize that the Chinese language they learn will definitely provide them with ample opportunities. So, I want them to experience China themselves and feel the cultural atmosphere of the country up close.

The destination that I chose was Yiwu City in Zhejiang Province. I wanted them to personally experience this city. Yiwu is a center for world trade; it's the world's biggest small product wholesale market and the world's "gold rush paradise" for buyers. Businesses and trading companies in over 100 countries and regions, including the USA, Germany, Italy, the Republic of Korea, the Middle East and Southern Asia, have representative offices in Yiwu, while business people from all over the world come here annually for the "gold rush."

In the summer of 2014, I brought over 40 students to the Yiwu International Trade Mart for the first time. It was exactly the year that phase II of the International Trade Mart opened and there was a special "business person area"—the Korean sector. A few thousand Korean business people were doing business here, seeing Yiwu as a chance to get themselves into the international market. Clothes from *Dae Jang Geum*, exquisite tableware, Korean specialty electronics were all exhibited in the Yiwu International Trade Mart.

At that time, the 40 or so students had just started to speak a few sentences in Chinese and didn't know much about China at all, and weren't even interested in the Yiwu trade experience, just thinking of it as a trip to China. I firmly believed though, that through this trade experience, the students would discover the massive potential for development that China has and would find that their future is undeniably linked to China.

Our journey to Yiwu was tough. The group first flew from South Korea to Shanghai and then had to get a bus from there to Yiwu, which took around three to four hours. As soon as we arrived, I brought the students to the International Trade Mart. When the students saw the mythical wholesale market which was said to be the largest in the world and the countless varieties of goods on display in the market, they were overwhelmed. Over the three days and two nights that we were there, the students experienced the Yiwu market, tried bargaining to buy different products and even sent what they had bought back to South Korea. Ever since we arrived there, the students were extremely busy and going non-stop, but the market was too big and three days were far from enough to see the whole thing.

From that year onwards, I brought students to the Yiwu Mart almost every year and each time I could see a big change. Now the trip to Yiwu has already become a routine practice as a part of experiencing the Chinese market. In 2017, they started flying direct from Seoul to Yiwu, so traveling to Yiwu has now become more convenient. The students did some comprehensive analysis on the business people of Yiwu and they found two main characteristics: the first was that the Chinese believe that "heaven rewards the diligent"—if you work hard, you will reap benefits; the second was that when the Chinese do business, they "see profits but are guided by righteousness"—you can't just focus on making profit, but also have to have good morals. We think that these two reasons are why Yiwu has been successful.

Recently, two of my students came back from Yiwu determined to start their own businesses and import products from Yiwu to sell in South Korea. For these students, the Yiwu trade experience has subtly changed their future. Yiwu is not just a place full of opportunities and challenges, but also a window to understanding China. In the future, I will continue to take my students to Yiwu and see the changes.

▼ A Walk through Yiwu to See the Changes

Travel

Slow and Fast: China Speed

Habib Aykal (Turkey)

I got back to Turkey in 2016 and took the high-speed rail from Ankara to Istanbul. It was great! I told everyone around me that this was the first high-speed rail that China had built overseas.

The An-Is high-speed rail is very popular. Since it was opened, the number of people traveling daily from Ankara to Istanbul by railway has increased from 4,000 to over 25,000.

In 2008, the first intercity railway with full independent intellectual property rights was opened between Beijing and Tianjin. Up to 2018, the total length

▼ Slow and Fast: China Speed

of the Chinese high-speed rail network had reached 25,000 km, which was 2/3 of the world's high-speed rail networks. The Chinese people have also allowed this technology to be exported and make traveling in other countries more convenient, for example, Turkey.

When my dad came to Beijing in 1980, the streets were packed with bikes; it was really a "kingdom of bikes." My dad said that at that time he took the old "green train" from Beijing to Shanghai, which didn't have any air conditioning and took over 20 hours. The China that my dad talked about was a simple and slow one, "Mr. Slow."

In 2012, my dad brought me to Beijing, which was my first time in China. The roads were full of private cars, taxis and buses. The metro, high-speed rail, planes, ships and maglev trains among other tools have provided different choices for travelers. Last year I went on the "Fuxing" high-speed train to Shanghai with my dad and it only took us less than five hours. The train carriage was clean and tidy, so it was an enjoyable experience. My dad was filled with many emotions.

My dad says that China will never again be the "Mr. Slow" that it was before. That said, China also has its "slow" aspects. For example, China's national treasure, giant panda, is called "half beat slow." When the Chinese eat, they

Travel

say "Please eat slowly." When they see people off, they say "Go slowly." If they encounter some problems when doing something, they say "Take your time." In textbooks, the exercise scene is one of slowly doing *taijiquan*, and in get-togethers, it's of slowly drinking tea. This type of easy and relaxed pace of life is also a part of Chinese life.

I like this kind of Chinese lifestyle. In speed there is slowness and in slowness there is speed. Chinese people practice *taijiquan* very slowly, but play table tennis very quickly; Chinese people practice calligraphy very slowly, but construct buildings very quickly; Chinese people drink tea very slowly, but do business quickly; Chinese people walk very slowly, but the high-speed rail they built is very fast.

▼ Slow and Fast: China Speed

Travel

Walking into a New Dawn on the First Rays of the Morning Sun

Carlos Abrego Escala
(Panama)

I am from Panama. Because of the tropical climate, I got into the habit of catching the sea breeze in the evenings before going to bed. Going to bed at midnight and getting up at 8:30 in the morning, I'd get some sort of breakfast and then go to school which was close by. This was always my lifestyle until I graduated with a master's degree and went home to find a job…

I had interviews at many multinational companies, but in the end, either the company didn't want me, or I wasn't satisfied with the salary they offered. In short, there was a long period of time when I couldn't find a satisfactory

Walking into a New Dawn on the First Rays of the Morning Sun

job and during this time, I was always complaining and losing my cool.

It was then that one of my friends told me that China Construction America was hiring new staff. My friend had already been for an interview, but hadn't passed because his Chinese wasn't good enough. He advised me to go for an interview because he knew my Chinese, English and Spanish were all very good. I told myself, "You've studied Chinese for so long and are obsessed with Chinese culture. Why not go and give it a try?"

The day of the interview was the first time I got up early. I walked into a new dawn on the first rays of the morning sun and for the first time, I appreciated that "an hour in the morning is worth two in the evening." The birds were singing in the trees, the leaves were dancing in the wind, and my heart was joyful and excited as I looked forward to a bright future. The interview went swimmingly. My ability to express myself in fluent Chinese and my sincere love of Chinese culture meant I was successful, and the Panama Office of China Construction America did not hesitate in taking me on.

A new season of my life began.

From the day of the interview onwards, that morning when I walked into the dawn on the first rays of the morning sun was engraved on my heart. The punctuality of my Chinese coworkers made the old, late-rising me become more efficient. Their unerring measurements in engineering dimensions, made the old, casual me more and more meticulous. The overtime they worked on weekends made me voluntarily join the overtime team. Even though the rest of the Panamanians "had enough money" and refused overtime, I think

that the time I spent with my Chinese colleagues working over the weekends was more meaningful and made my work skills improve more quickly.

I remember last year on the weekend leading up to New Year's Day, the manager asked our group to do a trend analysis of the money spent on buying materials over the previous six months and at the same time to estimate the costs for 2019. I was used to Excel, so normally whenever we had to produce any diagrams, it was me who did them. However, when the final product was typeset and printed, it was not quite artistic. The main reason was that I was not as used to the Chinese system of Excel as I was the Western language systems. When I told my Chinese colleague Li Wei about my struggles that weekend during overtime, without hesitating a moment, he took me step by step through how to use the Chinese Excel system. In less than an hour, a nice and neat chart was printed out. I was so happy! This would definitely not have been possible on a normal workday. On a normal workday, the office would have been too busy with people coming and going, phones constantly ringing, and everyone busy doing their own work. How would there be time to pay attention to anything else?

What surprised me most was the December 2018 tour of China. I went with the manager to the company headquarters to take part in three weeks of business training. The day we arrived in China, there was road construction next to the hotel, the wind was blowing hard and there was hardly anyone on the street. The next evening when I went downstairs, a smooth straight asphalt road busy with traffic met my eyes. What!? Am I dreaming? In Panama, they've been working on the road next to my house for a year already and it's still not completed! Seeing first-hand the speed of China made me even more obsessed with this great mystical country of the East.

Punctual and trustworthy, getting along harmoniously, quality first, and the pursuit of excellence... Now I finally realize why China has become the world's second largest economy within such a short period of time. It turns out that the people here all stick to these values and bury their heads in work...

I regret that I got to know China so late, but I'm proud to be part of the China Construction America team. Keeping my feet firmly on the ground, I will pave roads and build bridges for this country that gave birth to and provides for me, while also paving roads and building bridges of friendship between Chinese and Panamanian cultures.

I wake up every day with the first rays of sunlight, walking into the dawn, breathing in the sustenance of Chinese culture, and witnessing the take-off of Chinese science and technology. This kind of feeling is too wonderful for words.

An Experience of the Spring Festival Travel Rush

Thin Nandar Aye (Myanmar)

During the winter vacation in 2019, my classmates and I were not very eager to return home, and as well-seasoned foreigners, we planned to experience a Chinese "Spring Festival Travel Rush" at close range.

To this end, we specially researched the Spring Festival Travel Rush, as well as its background story. Originally, *chunyun*, the term for China's Spring Festival Travel Rush, first appeared in about 1980, and today it has approximately 40 years of history. For every person who is trying to make a living far from home, *chunyun* represents a longing for home, and reunion

▼ An Experience of the Spring Festival Travel Rush

with family. Since China's "reform and opening-up," [1] more and more people have chosen to leave their homes, going elsewhere for work or to pursue their studies. But, no matter how high they fly, or how far away they wander, they will always want to choose to go home for the celebration of the Spring Festival. Every year before and after the Spring Festival, China's bus stops, train stations, and airports are overcrowded with people. As time passes, this special "Spring Festival Travel Rush" phenomenon has taken form. Just imagine, every year during the month before and after the Spring Festival, nearly three billion trips are made across the country. What a spectacular event! From railways, to highways, to airplanes, every kind of traffic tool is set into maximum use, as thousands upon thousands of Chinese people all want to return home; the sheer logistics are truly impressive! What a both frightening and heart-warming phenomenon *chunyun* is! Frightening, because the size of the population in transit across the country is honestly almost too large to support, yet heart-warming due to the whole-hearted devotion Chinese people have in reuniting with their loved ones for the festival.

Our *chunyun* experience started in Beijing, with a goal to go to both Tianjin

---

[1] Reform and opening-up, *gaige kaifang* in Chinese, refers to China's economic reform and opening-up policies starting in 1978.

and Shijiazhuang. Even though the distance was not very long, we could still get a taste and feel of what the Spring Festival Travel Rush was like first-hand. We needed to buy train tickets from Beijing to Shijiazhuang, and we had heard that during China's *chunyun* period, even purchasing one ticket would be difficult to accomplish. In the past, one would need to go to many different train station ticket windows to wait in line; during peak times, one might wait as long as the entire day. Else, one could make non-stop calls on the phone in hopes of ordering tickets, and despite either of these efforts, still be unsure of getting a hold of any. Today, things are different, and China is fast in developing "Internet Plus." [1] Various apps make buying airplane tickets, train tickets, and even reserving hotel stays extremely convenient. We used our cellphones to download "Railway 12306," an official ticket-purchasing app, and after using our passports and names to register, we were able to get online and buy tickets. After succeeding in this purchase, we were even able to use "Railway 12306" to order our own meals for our trip on the high-speed rail. In the past, we had only heard of *A Bite of China*, an excellent Chinese gourmet food TV show, but this trip, with "Railway 12306," we experienced "A Bite of China on the High-Speed Rail," and it really was excellent!

On the high-speed rail, a family of three gave us the deepest impression. Their family's cheerful warmth, just smiling and talking with one another, really shared their joy and excitement in going home with us. They said, no matter how busy work got, every year during the Spring Festival, they would make time to go home to see their parents and close friends. The father arranged their luggage, the mother looked after their daughter, and the daughter kept feeding her mother and father goodies to eat; and she even gave us some to

---

[1] "Internet Plus" refers to the application of the Internet and other forms of informational technology in conventional industries. It is an incomplete equation where various internets can be added to other fields, fostering new industries and business development in China. It is China's version of Information Superhighway or Industry 4.0.

taste. They were so happy; that family's warm-heartedness and friendliness was infectious to all of us.

Something interesting is that in recent years, the ways in which Chinese people celebrate the Spring Festival have seen a change. This Spring Festival Travel Rush has seemed to start spreading to other countries and regions outside of China, up to the point that a lot of countries have a "Chinese Spring Festival Period." Why is this? Because during the Spring Festival vacation period, more and more Chinese families are choosing to travel abroad. Their footprints have spread over almost every popular tourist destination in the world, bringing a special "Chinese Spring Festival Period" to all of the world's "foreigners." My country Myanmar is no exception. After returning to Myanmar, my whole family went to Yangon's Chinatown to celebrate the Chinese Spring Festival. The street was decorated festively from end to end, with hanging red lanterns, auspicious Spring Festival couplets pasted on door frames, and food stands and restaurants all in the Chinese style. The only difference between us and Chinese people is that on the day of the Spring Festival, we didn't eat meat, but only vegetarian dishes. Even though there was no meat, the flavors and aromas were all very Chinese. In the evening, there was also a firework show, and the area was bustling with noise and excitement. In Yangon, I came across many Chinese visitors, most of whom were in whole families traveling together. In Yangon, they not only got to experience a vegetarian Spring Festival, but were also the bringers of this "Chinese Spring Festival Period" to our city, and it was extraordinarily lively.

The Chinese Spring Festival Travel Rush has changed in terms of the locations where people celebrate and the vacationing patterns, but what it has never changed, is the thousand-year tradition of familial ties and love that the Chinese people have always held sacred and will continue to cherish for years to come.

Tourism

Tourism

"If You Fail to Reach the Great Wall, Then You're Not a True Man"

Ifekpolugo Chinelo Mary-Juliet (Ye Wenji) (Nigeria)

Holo Louzolo Amandine (Ren Jing) (Republic of the Congo)

Ye Wenji: A few years ago, when I was learning Chinese at the Confucius Institute in Nigeria, we used a series of teaching materials called *Great Wall Chinese*, which had pictures of the Great Wall on the covers. Using *Great Wall Chinese*, I gradually learned Chinese and developed a yearning for China. From then on, I hoped I could learn Chinese well and visit the Great Wall one day.

Ren Jing: The Great Wall was the first thing I knew about China. I know

▼ "If You Fail to Reach the Great Wall, Then You're Not a True Man"

there is a famous Chinese saying: "If you fail to reach the Great Wall, then you're not a true man." And foreigners who haven't been to the Great Wall wouldn't be considered to have been to China.

Ye Wenji: Haha, yeah, as I wished, I have already become a "true man." I arrived in Beijing in September 2016. On an October morning, my friends and I got on a bus headed for Mutianyu Great Wall. During our trip, the guide said that Mutianyu was one of the most beautiful parts of the Great Wall and introduced us to a bit of the history. He told us that at that time, Emperor Qin Shihuang used the manpower of the whole country to build the Great Wall. Almost 300,000 people took part in this huge building project and some of them lost their lives in the process. The Great Wall is a symbol of the Chinese people's wisdom and strength spanning thousands of years.

Ren Jing: Exactly. It's hard to believe that, in an age when there was no machinery or means of transportation, people had to rely on their own hands to transport the bricks one by one up the steep mountains and stack them into a wall that has been standing for thousands of years.

Ye Wenji: The Great Wall is very long. It deserves its name, the "Ten-Thousand-*Li*[1] Great Wall"! We walked very far and caught our breath when we looked back at the amazing scene, and looking ahead, we could see the wall winding away into the distance. As we walked, we took in the scenery along the wall.

Ren Jing: For Chinese people, the Great Wall is a symbol of determination,

---

1 *Li* is a traditional Chinese unit of distance, now equal to 500 meter.

courage and strength. The so-called "true man," not only needs to reach the Great Wall, but must also be able to face the hardships on the way to achieving his dreams. When I need more strength or self-confidence, I go climb the Great Wall!

Ye Wenji: The tour guide told us that the original reason for building the Great Wall was for military defense. It can be traced back to the Western Zhou Dynasty, the Spring and Autumn period, and the Warring States period when they were at war with each other and had to defend against attack. This was the first stage of building, but the walls built then were all pretty short. After Emperor Qin Shihuang unified the country, he joined sections of the wall together and repaired them. People started calling it the "Great Wall." The Ming Dynasty was the last dynasty to work on the Great Wall, leaving us with the major part of the wall we see today.

It was autumn in Beijing the first time I went to the Great Wall. It was a bit cold, but the further I went, the happier I became and, in the end, I even started sweating. When did you go to the Great Wall?

Ren Jing: It was snowing the first time I went to the Great Wall. The wind blew the snow onto me and into my clothes, but I saw the unique beauty of the wall in the snow.

Ye Wenji: Now the Great Wall has new tourist facilities. You can walk one step at a time when going up, but choose to take the cable car when coming down.

Ren Jing: If we get the chance, we should go visit the Great Wall together!

▼ "If You Fail to Reach the Great Wall, Then You're Not a True Man"

The Imperial Palace: Growing Younger

Pakpoom Jainoi (Thailand)

In 2003, in Chiang Rai, Thailand, the adults and I were enchanted by a Chinese TV series that was popular in Southeast Asia—*My Fair Princess*. I was six years old that year. All the princesses in *My Fair Princess* were cute and lively, sincere and honest. My friends and I all loved Xiaoyanzi and Xia Ziwei. In Thailand, we also have a princess, Princess Sirindhorn, who is a China hand[1] and is really interested in its language and culture. Now many

---

1 This phrasing comes from the word 中国通, which has a deeper meaning than just expertness in the knowledge sense, but also in feeling, general attitude, and cultural understanding close to the level of a native.

▼ The Imperial Palace: Growing Younger

schools in Thailand offer Chinese courses.

I chose the Imperial Palace as my first stop in Beijing, which I had seen many times on TV. At last, when I was able to stand inside, I closed my eyes and thought back to all the times when I had looked forward to and imagined that moment. I felt so happy! Every room here, every tile, every ornament, every painting, and every piece of clothing is a period of history and each has its own story.

I slowly wandered through the palace, enjoying my surroundings and imagining the dignity of the emperor.

The buildings inside the Imperial Palace were very special. Not only were they magnificent, but also every tiny detail was exquisite. The four corners of every roof were turned up like the wings of a bird taking flight plus the dazzlingly eye-catching tiles. It was amazing! There is a park called Jingshan (Prospect Hill) Park at the back of the Imperial Palace, which used to be the emperors' royal garden. In Jingshan Park, I saw the ancient archways, the towering trees, and the blooming peonies. From the top of the hill, you could see the whole of the Forbidden City. It's hard to imagine that only the emperor used to be allowed there, when now anybody can spend all day in it for just 2 RMB. I saw many local elderly people dancing, playing chess, playing the *erhu* and singing Beijing opera. It was wonderful! All the royal gardens have been opened to the public. In Jingshan Park, I saw the wealthiness, generosity and dignity of the historical Beijing, and also the freedom, equality and acceptance of the modern city.

In the past few years, the Imperial Palace has become younger, and there is more "technological feel" to the place and the young people have welcomed the "Internet + Imperial Palace" project. From the solemn Forbidden City to "Weigugong" (Imperial Palace WeChat account) and an Imperial Palace Taobao shop, the Imperial Palace has become a part of people's lives in a fashionable way. I was enchanted by the "Weigugong" WeChat public account. By turning on my phone and going into the WeChat account, I could learn the story behind every item in the Imperial Palace and it was almost as if the items had come alive. The modern "Imperial Palace Cultural Creations" has given people many a pleasant surprise. The cultural creations use the cultural elements of the Imperial Palace to allow people to take home a piece of the fashionable culture with them. Before I went home for the winter vacation, I bought a whole bunch of "imperial travel" luggage tags and "palace gate plaque" fridge magnets for my Thai friends and family.

The reform and opening-up have allowed the seamless integration of tradition and technology. The 600-year-old Imperial Palace has also regained its youthfulness and relevance.

▼ The Imperial Palace: Growing Younger

Bridges—The Witnesses to Change

Anvesh Reddy (India)

I've been in China for over ten years. I really like this poem:

"I have been across many bridges,

Seen many clouds floating by,

Drunk many kinds of alcohol,

But only loved one woman of the right age."

The poem was written by Shen Congwen. In it, "bridges," "clouds," and "alcohol" are all enchanting, especially "bridges." What romantic structures with profound humanistic spirits!

Bridges—The Witnesses to Change

On weekends, I love to go walking along bridges.

When I first came to China in 2001, I went to visit Shijiazhuang and saw the Zhaozhou Bridge close by. I knew it was a famous Chinese stone arch bridge over 1,400 years old. Over the years, it has been buffeted by wind and rain, witnessing many disasters, but to this day, it still stands unscathed.

The bridge is a symbol of Chinese people's accumulated wisdom. Over the past ten-plus years, there has been an ever-increasing number of flyovers in Beijing. 立交桥 (flyover), what a good name! 立交 means "grade separation," which is a bridge that is built above road level that allows traffic on other routes to keep flowing without being disrupted. The different shapes and sizes of flyovers in China are magnificent and have left a great impression on me. Beijing has the most flyovers in China. The sight of all the majestic flyovers of all shapes rising above the city gives the city a modern feel.

On the 24th of October 2018, the HZMB was opened. The bridge is 55km long and joins Hong Kong, Zhuhai and Macao. It is the longest, most expensive and most complex sea-crossing bridge in the world.

I've already lived in China for over ten years. Over the years, Chinese bridges have allowed me to see changes. Now, every bridge that China constructs not only spans rivers and districts, but also joins cultures and hearts.

Tourism

Searching for the Chinese Dream

Tai Hsiao Hua (Malaysia)   Cao Huiqiong (China)

Cao Huiqiong: Hi, Ms. Tai! Welcome back to China! I'd like to ask what you think about China now? Compared with before, what are the most striking changes?

Tai Hsiao Hua: Over the years, China's economy, politics, culture and technology have all witnessed great changes. The most striking change compared with before is the way the fine culture has been passed down and developed.

Cao Huiqiong: Ms. Tai, in your book *Tai Hsiao Hua's Journey through China*, I noticed that you had been to the "fire pit" Turpan. What was your impression of the ancient city of Turpan when you were there?

▼ Searching for the Chinese Dream

Tai Hsiao Hua: I remember that Turpan is situated along the eastern half of the "Silk Road" on the western mouth of the Hexi Corridor and is an important hub for many travelers. In the old days, due to its superior geographical location, the ancient city was an important military town. People built cities to live in along the "Silk Road." The ancient buildings in the city reflect the intelligence, wisdom and creativity of the ancient laborers. Even today, the ruins of the ancient city still radiate the impressiveness of the days gone by.

Cao Huiqiong: Could you please talk about your understanding of the Chinese dream and what your own Chinese dream is?

Tai Hsiao Hua: For Chinese people, the Chinese dream is for the country to be strong and prosperous. My Chinese dream was only realized because one of my pieces of writing, *City Built in the Sand* (《沙城》), gave me the opportunity to visit China. It allowed me to find the homeland of my dreams, which is the homeland of my spirit—Chinese culture.

Cao Huiqiong: Could you talk about what China has impressed you the most in the past few years?

Tai Hsiao Hua: What has impressed me most is the "Belt and Road" initiative, which includes a lot of traditional Chinese cultural connotations and values, for example, harmony in diversity, common development, inclusiveness, valuing peace and harmony, etc. At the same time, the "Belt and Road" initiative revived the ancient "Silk Road," which has made China more open to the outside world. In this day and age, further development can only be achieved by opening up and embracing the cultures of the world. I believe that China will get better and better at this.

The "Sought-After Quintessence" in the Greater Bay Area

Vizer Rita (Hungary)

China's land is expansive, and its tourism scenery and resources are abundant. Many places are full of rich cultural meaning and historical significance. I have hoped that I might travel many of China's landscapes and see the wonders they hold. This year, I went to China's southern region in pursuit of this journey.

The Guangdong–Hong Kong–Macao Greater Bay Area is a world-class city group, including the two special administrative regions Hong Kong and Macao, as well as Guangzhou, Shenzhen, and Zhuhai among nine cities in Guangdong Province. I've heard that the Greater Bay Area has not only been

The "Sought-After Quintessence" in the Greater Bay Area

built as a world-class city group full of lively energy, but that it has been created as a high-class living circle where it will be enjoyable to live, work, and travel. The construction of the Hong Kong–Zhuhai–Macao Bridge (HZMB) has become an emblematic event of the Greater Bay Area. The enormous structure connects Guangdong Province's Zhuhai City to the Macao Peninsula, and links them to Hong Kong's Lantau Island. Since opening to traffic, travel time between the three destinations has been trimmed down to a mere 30 minutes at most.

The Greater Bay Area has a long and full history, a favorable climate, and rich markets for a variety of products and produce. The ancient and modern aspects beautifully reflect each other, while each of the cities' unique characteristics and features complement the group to create a colorful and brilliant whole. The "Pearl of the East" that is Hong Kong, the famous city of Macao whose roots are set far into the past, Guangzhou's hot springs and villages, Shenzhen's Window of the World theme park, Shunde's exquisite cuisine, and Zhaoqing's Seven-Star Crags, all made me wish to linger on in enjoyment, with no thought of ever tearing myself away or returning home.

During my travels, the Greater Bay Area drew me in with a deep fascination, and I fully believe that the megalopolis will become the future "sought-after quintessence" of many peoples of the world.

Leisure

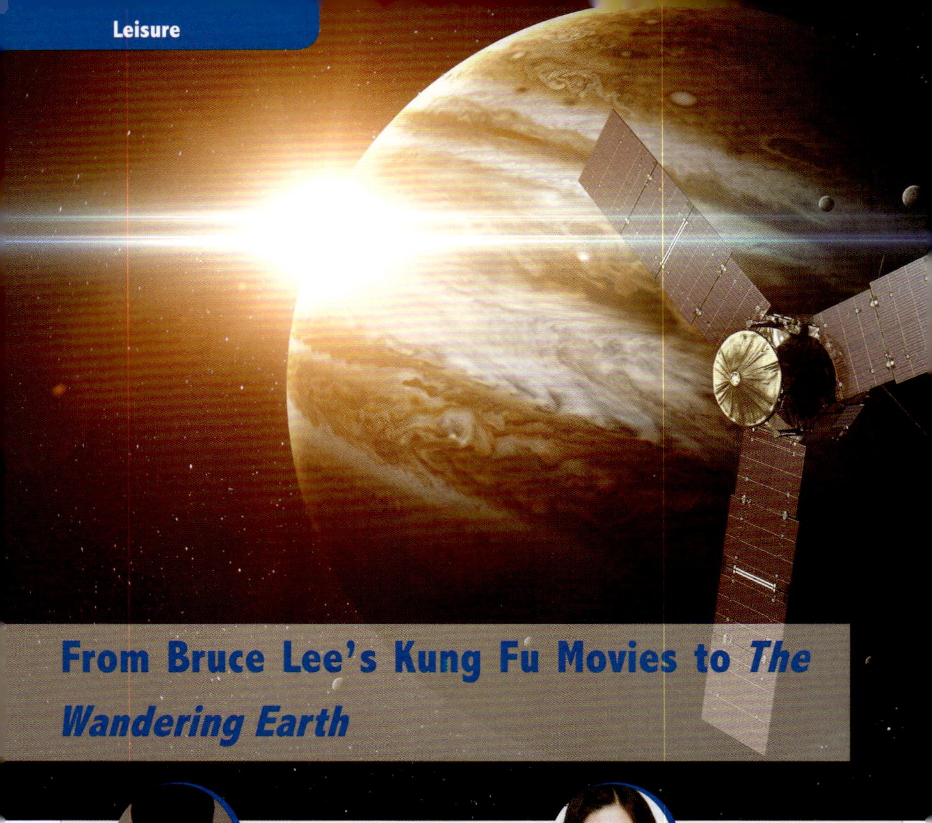

Leisure

From Bruce Lee's Kung Fu Movies to *The Wandering Earth*

Mike Sui (USA)

Wu Junyi (China)

Wu Junyi: Hey, Mike Sui! I'm so happy that I could meet you. While celebrating the Chinese New Year I saw the movie you starred in, *The Wandering Earth*. It was really great!

Mike Sui: Thank you! I feel greatly honored to have the opportunity to act in this movie. In this movie, everybody gets the chance to see my "Chinese heart," which is the most important to me.

Wu Junyi: You speak Chinese so well, even better than some announcers. People call you a "China hand." Have you lived in China since you were little?

▼ From Bruce Lee's Kung Fu Movies to *The Wandering Earth*

Or have you just spoken Chinese in the home growing up?

Mike Sui: I was born in America. My father is Chinese and my mother is American. When I was seven years old, I came with my mother to Beijing and began studying Chinese. In middle school, I moved back to America, but I missed China and longed for Beijing so much that I ended up returning here. I think that there is no better place in the world than Beijing, and it is where my roots are! I have many Chinese friends. I like using Chinese to communicate with them. I also really enjoy reading Jin Yong's Chinese novels, and like watching Chinese movies. All these things have greatly helped me with my Chinese studies.

Wu Junyi: Could you tell us some of your favorite Chinese movies?

Mike Sui: When I was little, I knew about Bruce Lee and I really liked to watch his kung fu movies. I felt that he was fierce and awe-inspiring in these movies' and made the Chinese kung fu spread all over the world. One of the reasons for China's kung fu movies' success in the international market is that they used kung fu to spread Chinese culture. Bruce Lee has already reached a legendary status. No matter what country you go to or what corner of the world you are in, if you say Bruce Lee's name, Chinese kung fu will immediately come to mind, and vice versa. After Bruce Lee's movies, Jackie Chan's kung fu movies are also very good. As Chinese kung fu movie endorsers, they showed the heroism in traditional Chinese culture through their movies, and opened a window to the world for understanding Chinese culture.

Wu Junyi: Yeah, Bruce Lee and Jackie Chan are known as the "Two Dragons." They've already become symbols of China to the world. *The Wandering Earth* has hit theaters internationally recently, and I've heard that it has had a quite good performance in North America. As one of the main actors, did you predict that it would achieve such a great success?

Mike Sui: Of course I thought it would do very well. As of April 2019, the worldwide box-office sales of *The Wandering Earth* had already grossed over $700 million (about 4.7 billion RMB) and it became the first movie in 2019 to earn over $500 million. *The Wandering Earth* has received very high ratings in reviews from around the world, and I think this positive reception can be attributed to a few main factors. Firstly, this movie is an adaption of Liu Cixin's science fiction novel of the same name, and the work combines natural disasters, technological progress, the universal predicament of human existence, and other similar grand main topics. The story manifests the power of science and nature and is brimming with the feeling of heroism. Secondly, our production team is incredibly sincere, meticulous, and professional. They specially wrote *The Wandering Earth*'s 100-year annalistic history for the story, drew several thousand schematic artwork drawings, and everyone on the working team was especially diligent. Everyone truly shot this movie so that it would shine as China's own science fiction movie and wanted to make the whole world see China's science fiction imagination and efficacy in this genre. So, in the end, the final product and results were very good. Finally, Wu Jing's participation, as well as all the talented actors' single-hearted effort, really gave this movie its own unique traffic.

Wu Junyi: How is this movie different from other Chinese movies that you have encountered?

Mike Sui: There are so many differences. Most Chinese movies before were about love, family, or crime, or comedies. You would very rarely find any of the science fiction variety. Right now, China's economy is developing rapidly, and technology is more and more sophisticated. Chinese people's communication with foreigners is becoming more frequently. Ideas are colliding, more and more people have the conditions and bravery to shoot many different kinds of movies, and they are very passionate in their work. This kind of experimentation and dedication will surely bring about a breakthrough in Chinese film-making.

Wu Junyi: This movie has certainly given a lot of people hope and has helped to make a lot more people steadfast in pursuing their own dreams in the movie industry. It has helped them to believe that one day, Chinese movies will gain approval and acclaim from the whole world.

Mike Sui: *The Wandering Earth* is only a beginning. I believe that after a lot of people have seen it, they will be encouraged and inspired to work hard and exert greater effort towards accomplishing their movie dreams. They will keep on showing the power of Chinese movies.

Leisure

"Ambassador" Tchiegue's "Face-painted Life"

Francis Tchiegue
(Cameroon)

Hou Yuqing (China)

Hou Yuqing: Hello, Mr. Tchiegue! You are often seen on the screens of Chinese television, and I'm very glad to meet you today! Your official introduction says that you can speak Chinese, English, French, German, Russian, Italian, Spanish, and the list goes on to more than ten languages. Furthermore, you are skilled in hosting live events, crosstalk, "face-changing,"[1] Peking opera, and singing... and in addition, you've already

---

1 Face-changing, or *bianlian*, is a special performing art in which the performer switches masks at a rapid speed, in such a way that it appears to give off the illusion of magic-use.

got your doctorate degree in mathematics in Cameroon and have a secure position in the United Nations. How was it that you began your journey in China?

Francis Tchiegue: Because my father was a kung fu devotee, ever since childhood, my yearning to learn about and curiosity towards Chinese culture had been nurtured and encouraged under his influence. When I was 25, I used to live a stable life in Cameroon. But a Chinese-Cameroonian governmental scholarship for an exchange student program aroused my "Beijing Dream" buried deep within my heart. Beijing is the capital of Chinese culture, and is the "most Chinese" city in the world, so I came here. My first stop in Beijing was Beijing Language and Culture University, and starting from the fundamental basics, I began my studies in Chinese. After a year of study, I transferred to Beihang University to diligently pursue my doctorate studies in computer technology, but I was still most infatuated with Chinese language and culture.

Hou Yuqing: Yes, I have also seen you perform *pingshu* (a traditional folk art form of storytelling) on television before, and it was really amazing!

Francis Tchiegue: Chinese language and culture are so very interesting! If I were unable to unravel and master the workings of the language, there would have always been a mountain-like barrier separating myself from Chinese culture and my beloved Beijing style, and even the activities of my daily life would have had their own difficulties. Once, I saw Canada's Dashan perform crosstalk on television with Ding Guangquan and thought to myself: "How great it would be if I could speak Mandarin with such authenticity like them!" I decided to turn to Ding Guangquan and acknowledge him as my teacher. From then on, I had practiced tricky traditional theatrical pieces that he provided me with every day, and kept practicing until I reached the kind of level I am at now.

Hou Yuqing: Your versatility and talents are astonishing! Peking opera and "face-changing" are two of your particularly unique talents. For so many years you have been enlivening China's stages and television screens with your brilliant work. From your 2012 Spring Festival singing of *Face-painted Life* on Hunan TV, to the Spring Festival Gala on Beijing TV, and Anhui TV's theater-centered Spring Festival program, you've already become a frequent guest on many TV stations' Spring Festival activities. You've been considered an old friend of the Chinese *quyi*[1] fans for a long time now, and are very popular among the Chinese people.

Francis Tchiegue: China's traditional opera is time-honored, wide-ranging, and profound. Even though a foreigner like me has attempted to show off my amateur opera performances in front of many true experts in the field, my fervor for traditional Chinese opera has not diminished in the slightest. The next steps I would like to take, if given the opportunity, would be to go on CCTV's Spring Festival Gala and perform Chinese opera.

Hou Yuqing: Surely you will. I look forward to it!

Francis Tchiegue: When foreigners arrive in China, the first things they see are high-rises, large buildings, and large bridges..., but what I wish most is that I could take them to see Beijing's *hutongs*, that they would see some of the true traditional China. I would like to take them to Beijing's Chang'an Grand Theater, for them to see some plays, to see Peking opera, Huangmei opera[2], Henan opera, Shaoxing opera, and so on. I'd like to take them to see

---

1 *Quyi* refers to traditional Chinese art forms such as ballad singing, storytelling, crosstalk, etc.
2 Huangmei opera is a traditional, local operatic form in Anhui Province.

jingyun dagu, a Beijing storytelling event with the sonorous booming of drum accompaniment.

Hou Yuqing: You have a kind of perseverant, diligent, and hard-working spirit that others cannot parallel, that is firm and indomitable. The contributions that you have made towards Chinese-Cameroonian cultural communication have been very great over the years.

Francis Tchiegue: I don't have such a clear objective, but I know that my forward direction is pointed towards cultural communication. I hope that the peoples of the world will develop increasingly greater mutual understanding for each other. I hope we will be able to say that though we are different in skin color, cultural background, and religious belief, we can still cooperate with each other, and live together peaceably; and we will recognize each other as one global family.

I Want to Star in the Spring Festival Gala

Ka Kyosei (Japan)

Ever since I was little, I have been a bundle of joy to my family. I would frequently perform a mini program at all of our family gatherings, and slowly, I developed a confident and forthright personality. From elementary school to senior high school, I had always been our school's star in the arts; performing arts activities of all types and lengths could never be found without my hand in them. When I was four, I started to study Chinese, and I was interested in all the performing arts activities related to China.

I know, in China, the most important performing arts program is the CCTV Spring Festival Gala on the eve of Chinese New Year. Almost all Chinese

people in the world will circle around in front of the TV, enjoying this end of the year arts program and feast. I also know that China's Spring Festival Gala has always been a very open stage, and there is no lack of international faces or of grass-roots stars on that stage.

In 1988, the stage of the Spring Festival Gala saw its first foreign face to appear on the program—Yugoslavia's Ka'erluo (*transliteration*), and after this there were Canada's Dashan, Argentina's Hillel Gitter, Cénadian singer Céline Dion, French actress Sophie Marceau, and so on. Their appearances on the Spring Festival Gala added a new element and injected fresh blood into the viewing experience. I remember there was a small skit called *Tongxi Tongle* (*Everybody Celebrating Together*), in which an African girl spoke Chinese fluently, and in so few words revealed the extent of the outstanding friendship between China and African countries. I also remember a special performance of the song *I Love You, China*, in which the performers were an international youth choir from different countries around the world expressing their love for China through their singing. Hearing their resounding and impassioned voices, I couldn't avoid tears welling up in my eyes. I really wished that I could charge through the screen, and join together with them in the song—if I could only stand on that stage, that would've been wonderful beyond words!

With such a dream in mind, I worked very diligently in my Chinese studies, and worked hard to improve my accomplishments in the arts. My major was in broadcasting and hosting—using Chinese! I've had my voice heard before on CCTV-1's *AI vs Human*, CCTV-4's *Our Chinese Heart* and other programs, as well as been a voice-over during the 2017 Belt and Road Forum.

Leisure

Amid my day-to-day work, I've deeply experienced the fast development of China, and at the same time, I am also very proud that I might be a part of it, and a witness to it. However, I am not wholly satisfied with the level I have risen to, and I still haven't stopped my forward pace. My dream to be in the Spring Festival Gala still remains. My desire to ascend onto that grandest stage and to show my talents and skills to everyone still pushes me onward.

I have many interests and hobbies. I can sing Peking opera: one of my favorite verses is "Love and hate both exist in but a moment…" from *The Drunken Concubine*, which tells the love story of Yuji and Xiang Yu and is so full of twists and turns that I've sung it over and over. I also like to dub films; CCTV has many programs that feature my dubbed voice. I also like calligraphy: I've written "东海西海，心理攸同；南学北学，道术未裂" (Eastern Sea and Western Sea, my heart is one with both; I've studied South and studied North, the Way is broken not), which sixteen characters are the philosophical idea that I hold on to in my studies. Poetry recitation is also a favored past-time of mine: "撑一支长篙，在青草更青处漫溯……" (To pole a boat upstream, to where the green grass is most verdant and flows along the water edge…), which gives me a boldness that springs only from a mind full of the breath of Confucian classics…

My favorite author is Lin Haiyin. Both Lin Haiyin and I were born in Japan, and later moved to Beijing. While living in Beijing, Lin Haiyin was still a child, so she writes Beijing through the eyes of a child and sees Beijing as her nursing mother watching over her. When reading *My Memories of Old Beijing*, I truly felt the author's warm love for Beijing. When I came to Beijing, I had already grown up, but as I walked through the *hutongs* of Beijing and heard the laughter of little children ringing through the *hutongs*, I recalled Yingzi in *My Memories Old Beijing* and the corners of my mouth couldn't help but curl into a small smile of remembrance.

▼ I Want to Star in the Spring Festival Gala

"Home is where the heart is." In the blink of an eye, I've already been in China for eight years. Not only have I gained a lot of knowledge, but I have also found love. In 2018, I married a girl from Shanxi, and I've gone from a foreign student to a genuine Chinese son-in-law. China took on my poems and distant origins, and in return gave me a stage on which to chase my dreams and provided me with the opportunity to bring those dreams to realization, and then, even gave me a family.

"We are all diligently running our race, and we are all dreamers in pursuit of our dreams." While chasing my dreams, I believe that my dream of starring in the Spring Festival Gala will come true one day.

Leisure

My Chinese Dream and Chinese Family

Suleeporn Suebsiriviriyakorn
(Thailand)

Since I was young, I've grown up in a Thai family inundated with Chinese culture. Every day I would hear *Tianmimi*[1], one of my father's favorite songs, and saw my mother's beloved Chow Yun-fat[2]. Gradually, a dream linking to China took root in my heart and began to grow—I wanted very much to go to that country and see it for myself.

---

1 See page 24.
2 Chow Yun-fat is a Chinese actor from Hong Kong, who has been active since 1973, and is best-known in the West for his roles in *Crouching Tiger, Hidden Dragon* and *Pirates of the Caribbean: At World's End*.

At the age of 19, I was recommended for admission to Chiang Mai University's Chinese Department. I'd been working hard non-stop, and I felt like I had this vision of the future in my mind: China was just ahead of me waiting. In my second year of college, my school organized a Chinese culture day, and I performed Chinese calligraphy. At the time, there were many visitors who attended our activity. A very kind Chinese boy sat in front of me and watched for a very long time. Though he told me that he wasn't very good at calligraphy, he still gave me some slight direction and encouragement on my calligraphy work. Afterwards, we continued to keep in contact by letter, and even though we were very far apart from each other, we felt that our hearts were being drawn closer and closer, and gradually, this young Chinese man became my boyfriend. With him by my side, I felt like my blurry Chinese dream was becoming clearer and clearer.

In 2012, I went to my boyfriend's hometown—Tongchuan, Shaanxi—for the first time. Even today, I still remember, the moment his father saw me, he immediately came up to me and took my hand saying: "Are you tired? Hungry? Quickly come inside and eat!" At the moment, I was stunned. I'd studied Chinese for such a long time, yet I still really couldn't understand his Shaanxi accent. Of course, I couldn't understand even one sentence. At the time, I could only express my respect for them through my smile. During the few days of my stay, every day people would come to see me, this "foreign wife." I also sort of learned a few silly sentences in Shaanxi dialect: "他大舅他二舅都是他舅，高桌子低板凳都是木头"[1] (His first uncle and second

---

[1] This silly phrase is somewhat of a tongue twister in Chinese, and is comparable to a nursery rhyme of sorts.

uncle, both are his uncles; a high table and a low bench are both made of wood). Every time I said this sentence to them, they would all laugh aloud, and make me say it several times, laughing again and again each time. Even though I couldn't understand the Tongchuan dialect very well, I could still tell that they liked me from their expressions and they made me feel at home. They even took me to Shaanxi's cave dwellings, and I was able to walk around the cave, taking the sight of it all in, and truly experience it. I thought I was very lucky: not even every Chinese person will ever get to see those caves with their own eyes, much less a foreigner. Just remembering those kinds of unique and special places in my heart wasn't enough; I wanted to share them with my friends and family in another country! On the day when I left, the whole family saw me off, and they also gave me a little red envelope[1], and put together some food and drink in case I were to get hungry or thirsty on my way. I got in the car, and my eyes were already welling up. I couldn't say anything, but could only tearfully wave goodbye. Even while I've been far away in Thailand, from being awarded first place in my school's calligraphy competition to winning second place in the Thailand Chinese Bridges competition, they have continued to encourage and support me.

Now, I'm already attending Communication University of China, studying for my doctorate in broadcasting. Once I got my PhD acceptance letter, my fiancé and I got married. During the Spring Festival this year, I went back to Tongchuan again to celebrate the Chinese New Year. This time, I have had a strong feeling that, this is my home!

As for my Chinese dream, I started out in the beginning but with no end in sight. It was awoken from a faint hope to set my feet on the land of China to me being the wife of a Chinese man, which has been a wonderful experience of more than ten years. As I look forward to the next 10 years, 20 years, and

---

1 The little red envelope, or *hongbao*, is a small gift of money commonly given as a present in China, especially during holidays or special occasions.

▼ My Chinese Dream and Chinese Family

30 years, perhaps I will have even more dreams that spring up from China and even more stories to tell in this beautiful country. My sweetheart is in China, my family is in China, and my children will also be in China. China is the place I dreamed of visiting as a child, now it is my future home, and I will bring my dreams along with me and let them fly in the country.

Leisure

Yao Ming: China's Symbol Venturing in the NBA

Calunjinji Rita Dicacia César (Russia)

Calunjinji Rita Dicacia César (Angola)

Saratov Bislan (Kazakhstan)

Claire Bing-Xin Boquet (France)

Hou Yuqing (China)

Baek Changhun (Republic of Korea)

Yao Ming: China's Symbol Venturing in the NBA

Bing-xin: In 2008, during the Beijing Olympics, I was 15 years old, and my family and I were watching the Beijing Olympics opening ceremony. Yao Ming held a child's hand and led the Chinese Olympic team into the arena. It left a very deep impression on me. My father even asked, "Is that little boy Yao Ming's son?"

Alina: I also saw the live broadcast, and we all thought that the child was very lucky, having the chance to hold hands with Yao Ming and bear the national flag in the opening ceremony.

Hou Yuqing: That little kid was a young hero named Lin Hao, who was a recent earthquake survivor. On May 12, 2008, China experienced the Wenchuan Earthquake. At the moment of the earthquake, the little nine-year-old Lin Hao rushed into the ruins to rescue his classmates. At the time, he was the youngest hero to help the earthquake survivors. Yao Ming and Lin Hao bore the national flag hand in hand.

Baek Changhun: Oh! So that is the actual story! An athlete and a young hero! Actually I'm a basketball fan and I like Yao Ming very much.

Bislan: His personality on the court is both humorous and relaxed, and he seems easy and amiable to approach, which made him very popular among the basketball fanbase, and he quickly became one of the NBA stars. "Yao Ming," this name has already become a symbol of China; when he is mentioned, we often say "China Yao."

Anvesh Reddy: He really is very humorous. I remember back in the 2004 Athens Olympics opening ceremony, Yao Ming announced an explosive vow that if the Chinese National Basketball Team was unable to get to a quarter-

final, he would not shave for half a year.

Alina: I knew this, and afterwards he shaved his beard, haha!

Hou Yuqing: In the summer of 2002, Yao Ming became the first Chinese basketball player to enter the NBA as a first overall pick. After that, the "Little Giant" Yao Ming became one of the most popular Chinese symbols and NBA idols. The NBA has added many Chinese elements. Beginning in Yao Ming's era, the NBA arena started to show many commercials for Chinese brands. Especially whenever there was an important Chinese holiday, such as the Spring Festival, the Lantern Festival, and the Mid-Autumn Festival, performers would be invited to the arena whereas originally only Chinese communities would have performances to celebrate these events.

Rita: In the domain of Chinese and American cultural interaction, Yao Ming is the greatest "export" from China to America. The NBA has deepened its expansion into the Asian markets and its commercial value has increased greatly.

Baek Changhun: I think that Yao Ming represents a new image for the

Chinese people. Traditional Chinese people are industrious and brave, friendly and modest, while Yao Ming not only possesses the traditional disposition of Chinese people, but also has modern characteristics. He is quick-witted, humorous, and full of creativity and confidence.

Business

From a Sales Champion to an Entrepreneur

Andrew Gatera (Rwanda)

In 2004, when I was 18, I entered into Airtel Africa, the largest telecommunications company in Africa, similar to China Mobile. While with Airtel Africa, I was responsible for marketing and retail services, principally business transactions concerning cellphones and other telecommunications products. I worked there four years, for three of which I was awarded the annual "Best Salesperson" award. At that time, what I sold best were Chinese cellphone products, including Chinese cellphone chargers, portable chargers, cellphone cards, and other such telecommunications commodities. Before

▼ From a Sales Champion to an Entrepreneur

long, I had opened my own franchise store, employed approximately 13 staff members, and apportioned five motorbikes for delivering telecommunications products to customers. ZTE cellphones were in very high demand in my country; Ugandans had a liking for Chinese brands, and especially liked buying ZTE electronic equipment. Soon, I was riding the wave of this investment, and had made a great fortune off it. To reward my efforts, I bought myself an off-road vehicle. Every day I would take it for a spin and was very pleased with myself and my accomplishments.

After I had gained all this, I started to turn my attention to something different, such as, why China's telecommunications business was so well developed and what kind of mysterious nation it was. In January 2010, I called my parents, and told them I wanted to travel to China and get a feel for the distant country. Fortunately, they gave me their full support, saying that if I wanted to go, I should go. Without hesitation, I set out from Uganda, boarded a plane bound for Beijing, and stayed there for the next six years of my life.

In February 2010, when I was 24, I started studying Chinese from scratch, and began my life at the Communication University of China. My studies and life in Beijing were very happy. Besides studying Chinese language and culture, I also learned how to make Beijing roast duck, and was elected as an ambassador in popularizing the dish worldwide. I also acknowledged a Master Magician as my instructor in the ways of Chinese magic and mastered my training to such a level that I was able to perform in TV magic programs.

Business

After receiving my bachelor's degree, I continued to pursue a master's degree in MTCSOL (Master of Teaching Chinese To Speakers of Other Languages).

After graduating with my master's, I decided to return to Rwanda, my home country, as an entrepreneur. My life and studies in China had broadened my horizon. Rwanda's unique history, culture, and natural environment gave me a very good platform for starting up in entrepreneurship. After a separation of six years, when I returned home, I was pleasantly surprised to discover that Rwanda and China's Alibaba Corporation had founded Africa's first worldwide electronic commerce platform together. Alibaba's Jack Ma was my idol!

I decided to set up a travel agency devoted to the Chinese market. With relations between China and Rwanda being very good, and my superb Chinese language skills, my company (G-STEP TOURS "www.gsteptours.com") was established with ease and very quickly set on a smooth and steady track of operation. Many Chinese tourists have come through my company when traveling to Rwanda, which made me very excited. In Rwanda, I have

▼ From a Sales Champion to an Entrepreneur

received many Chinese travelers, and they gasp in surprise whenever they hear my fluent Beijing dialect. It makes them willing to accept my company's services, and even introduce me to more Chinese tourists who want to visit Rwanda in the future. I feel so happy! Chinese has donned me with the wings of my dreams and made my entrepreneurship venture one of favorable winds and smooth sailing!

In 2018, my e-commerce platform UMUJYI.COM was chosen by Alibaba Corp; my team, together with Rwanda's other entrepreneurs, went to Hangzhou and received specialized training at Alibaba headquarters. I've been very fortunate, to have received personal instructions from Jack Ma and his colleagues. From this, I believe that my business will truly take off. My dreams are approaching reality, and my secret is—Chinese language and China!

Smart Life in Beijing

Christian Tabouguia
Kamgaing (Cameroon)

In the fall of 2011, when I graduated from college, I suddenly realized that Cameroon had so many Chinese people! They were there building Cameroon's railways, starting up companies, managing factories, and opening Chinese restaurants… They were awfully busy. It made me think of a saying: "Where there is seawater, there are Chinese; where there are Chinese, there are Chinese characters!" So, I decided to start studying Chinese, with the hope that one day, I might go to China to travel around and see it for myself. I like singing, and the four tones of Chinese, *yinping*, *yangping*,

Smart Life in Beijing

shangsheng, qusheng[1], seem just like a lovely melody flowing to my ears, an absolute delight to hear.

Hard work pays off. In September 2016, after a 15-hour plane ride, I finally landed in Beijing Capital International Airport. The airport is so huge! The modernized design really took my breath away. On my way from the airport to my university, I couldn't stop taking pictures as mementos; even today, it is fresh in my mind as if it were yesterday. While living in Beijing, every day was full of new and vitalizing experiences. The first time I came to a Chinese subway station and saw the sea of people, at that very moment, I had a particular feeling that the number of people in any of China's big cities' subway stations seemed to be the equivalent of Cameroon's entire population!

As a student studying abroad in China, I was very lucky to have chanced upon this new age of China! Here, there is a particular kind of lifestyle known as "Full Wifi Coverage." No matter where you go, you can receive a signal, and most important is that mobile data is incredibly cheap—every month I have leftover data. This kind of Internet service is great for foreigners who live in this new Chinese era. We don't need to go to the bank to exchange money, because almost everything can be easily arranged using a smartphone. Life here is incredibly convenient. To shop at a supermarket, one need only turn to the shop assistant with their WeChat QR code to scan and pay, and it removes the trouble of searching around for change. If I want to buy something, but am too lazy to go out, I can simply pick up my cellphone

---

1 *Yinping, yangping, shangsheng*, and *qusheng* are respectively the 1st, 2nd, 3rd, and 4th tones in Mandarin Chinese.

to browse Tmall Supermarket and place the order, and they will send the products directly to my door... This convenience struck me most at the time when I first came to China. In Cameroon, all the four seasons of the year are summertime, so when I arrived in north China, I was not used to the cold winter. I wanted to buy an outer coat, so I opened Taobao[1], entered in my desired size and style, and very quickly was able to buy the kind of clothing that suited my taste. When I wanted to eat, I also didn't need to brave the cold to go to a cafeteria, but just picked up my cellphone to order a take-out from Meituan, Ele.me, or Baidu Take-out[2]; almost any kind of delicacy could be found. When a delivery guy brought me this kind of good food, it seemed like "a fire in the winter," a pool of warmth! I think that I've truly been leading an easy life with everything provided!

China's integration of smart technology into their living has given me a life with endless possibilities! My classmates and I once interviewed fellow Cameroon countrymen in China, asking them: "Once you leave China, what do you think you will miss the most?" Their answers successively were: Taobao, Ele.me, and Baidu Take-out. Truly, these applications and platforms of the smartphone have made us feel the convenience that speedy Internet development has brought to our daily life. Now, I have "followed the local customs." I hope one day people back home will also have such a comfortable and convenient life.

Now, China is embracing an era of sharing economy, under which we only need to spend very little money and we can share some daily items: shared offices, shared bikes, shared cars, even shared strollers, and shared children's toys in shopping malls and parks. Truly, in this age, "there is only what

---

1 Taobao is a website for online shopping.
2 Meituan, short for Meituan-Dianping, is China's largest service-focused e-commerce platform. Ele.me is a food-ordering delivery service, and is linked to Baidu Take-out, another such service.

▼ Smart Life in Beijing

cannot be imagined and nothing that cannot be done." Among these shared goods, shared bikes have already become commonly used by us foreigners living in China. Bike riding on China's large streets and small alleys allows you to feel the pulse of history, enjoy modern technology, and experience the new era of China. It is really a wonderful feeling beyond words!

Business

"Made in China" and the Perceptions Thereof

Joo Jeonghun (Republic of Korea)

Majid Shaker (Iran)

Taniguchi Yukiyo (Japan)

Ogbuigwe Opral-Blessed (Nigeria)

▼ "Made in China" and the Perceptions Thereof

Joo Jeonghun (Republic of Korea)

In recent years, China's reflection can be found in almost every corner of the world, especially on products that were "Made in China." From a very early time until now, South Korea has continuously been subject to the influence of this huge neighbor country. When I was little, the impression that Chinese products gave us was: prices were almost unbelievably low, but the quality was also unimaginably poor. If we bought anything and it broke after one use, we didn't pay attention to where the product was actually produced, but would still always say: "This must be a Chinese product." At the time, "Made in China" became synonymous with poor quality.

But now? The situation is already very different. Xiaomi[1] was the first company to begin overturning Koreans' old impression towards the "Made in China" label. From cellphones to chargers, cordless earbuds as well as handbags, all these products have a fairly nice quality-price ratio, and have gained popularity, especially among young Koreans in pursuit of fashionable products.

More and more "Made in China" products are increasingly changing our perception of China. "Made in China" is no longer used as a byword for "cheap goods." Along with China's rapid economic development, China is expected to become the largest base where new products are developed and manufactured. I really look forward to the next step China will take in turning the whole world's eyes on it in amazement.

---

1 Xiaomi is a Chinese electronics company founded in 2010.

Business

Majid Shaker (Iran)

Many foreigners think that any product imported from China has both low price and cheap quality, but I see otherwise after I came to China. Shopping on Taobao is a good example of this. I can search for the kinds of items I want to buy and will find that there are many retailers and stores to choose from, and there are many different prices. I've tried this many times and confirmed the philosophy that "you get what you pay for" when it comes to higher and lower pricing. If I want a product of the best quality, I can't have the mentality of going after the lowest possible price. But, even if it is Taobao's "high price," in comparison to that in my country, I would still consider it a "low price."

So, I think that China has all manner of different kinds and qualities of products, and each can buy according to their own individual needs. It certainly isn't the case that all "Made in China" products are cheaply manufactured. You just need to be willing to spend a little extra, and you can buy goods of the best quality in China.

Taniguchi Yukiyo (Japan)

In the past, most Japanese people thought that, although China's products were very cheap price-wise, their quality was terrible. As a result, some Japanese did not really trust goods manufactured in China. However, with the development of China, this situation has seen a great change.

As China's research and development capacity has increased, the goods that Japan imports from China have become more and more advanced, and the technology content is also increasingly high. Furthermore, what has pleasantly surprised me is that the functions of Chinese products are so diverse and strong. In Japan, for the same price, you can only buy a product with one function, whereas in China, this product may possess five different functions. Because of this, I've come to truly admire the creativity of Chinese manufacturers.

Ogbuigwe Opral-Blessed (Nigeria)

In Nigeria, products made in China have been received with welcome. Our large cities each have their own Chinatown. If you want to buy something for a low cost, you'd better go there. But the only pity is that many of the goods' quality is rather poor. But with Chinese economic development, goods "Made in China" have also seen a tremendous improvement. The products made in China are rich in variety, from the small commodities of food and clothing, to large-scale living and transportation, including cars, bridges, railways—they have everything! In Lagos, Nigeria's largest city, the light rail was manufactured by China, and the minibuses also bear the "Made in China" label. In the future, I hope that China will be able to expand and develop their national brands, so that the whole world will look at the "Made in China" label with new eyes.

"Made in China" certainly isn't a label which remains unchanged. With the development of China's economy, science and technology, this label will experience quantitative change, and finally qualitative change. China will go from leading simply in manufacturing, to being a leader in innovation and product creativity.[1]

---

[1] In Chinese, the word for manufacturing (制造, zhìzào) is pronounced the same as a word coined for innovation (智造, zhìzào). It is a goal for China to make a transition from one *zhizao* to the other, to go from primarily manufacturing to making great leaps in the innovative market.

Business

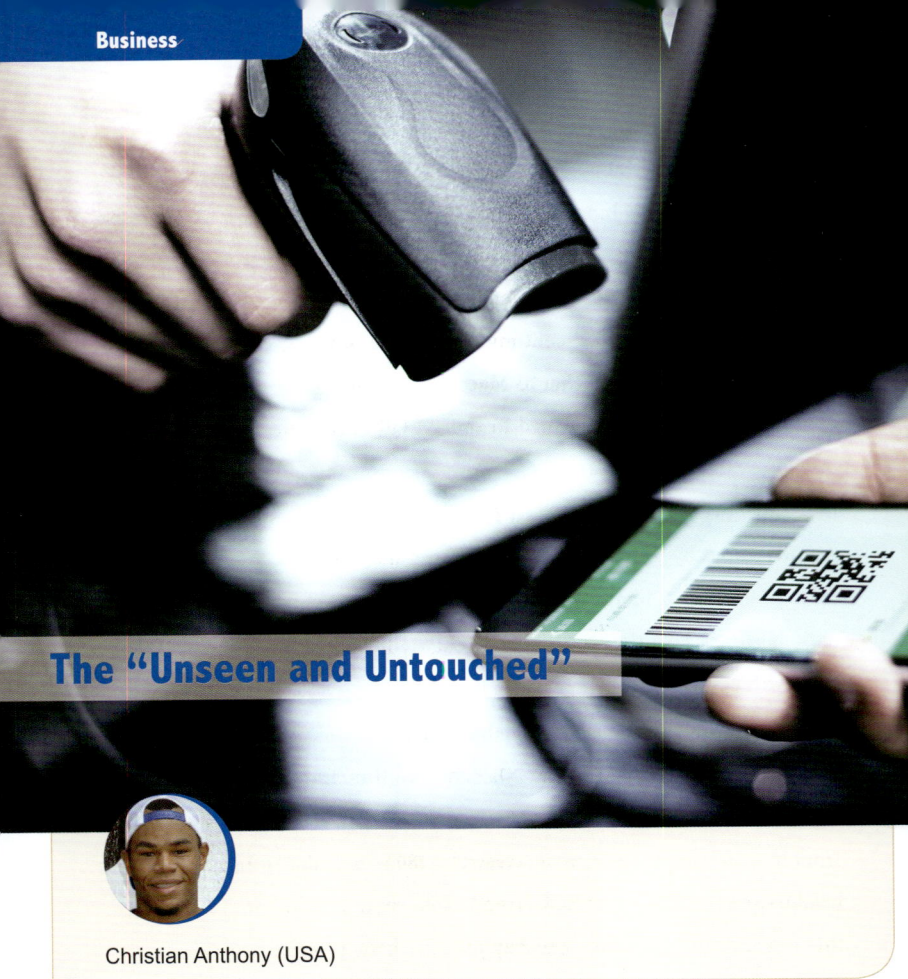

The "Unseen and Untouched"

Christian Anthony (USA)

What is "unseen and untouched"? The first dollar I spent in Beijing was on a bottle of Nongfu Spring mineral water. WeChat, the well-known app, helped me complete this transaction. Just outside of Jianguomen Subway Station, I used my cellphone to scan the QR code and pay the shopkeeper the fee. But throughout this process, I neither saw nor touched a cent of the money paid.

Before I came to Shanghai, many of my friends told me that China had a new payment method—mobile payment. With WeChat Pay or Alipay, buying things is especially convenient and fast. Whether you want to buy fruit, clothes, or a car, you can finish the purchase effortlessly in the blink of an eye.

The "Unseen and Untouched"

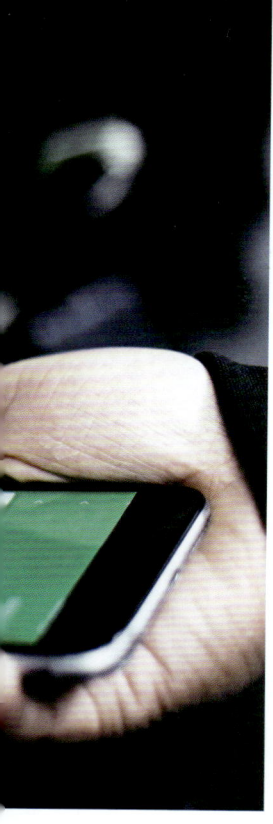

Like a lot of other Americans, the first time I came to China, I was very surprised. I didn't expect that in the other part of the world, mobile payment was so speedy and convenient. Soon, I began to try this new mode of payment myself, such as buying a plane ticket from Shanghai to Macao or a buffet-style lunch, for each I only needed to show a QR code, and the purchase was done.

Over the past few decades, the patterns of consumption have seen a huge change around the world; and compared with other parts of the world, China has undergone a particularly impressive change in its mode of payment. In less than 10 years, mobile payment has become prevalent in China. A data report WeChat released in 2017 showed that on average, 902 million users logged on WeChat daily and WeChat offline payment increased by 280%. In China, some people even have their salaries transferred directly into their WeChat accounts. Using this mode of payment, one can buy plane tickets, pay their child's tuition, and even invest in stocks. Yet such large amounts of money are "unseen and untouched" by the people paying them, which is almost unbelievable.

In the United States, no matter whether I spent one dollar on snacks, or fifty dollars on groceries, the cashier would always give me back my change, and sometimes a receipt as well; in China, I seldom use cash. Once, my friend and I challenged to spend an entire month without using cash, and we both easily passed the challenge.

I really like the convenience of this "unseen and untouched" mobile payment.

Business

Shanghai—A City of Hope

Tjibbe van Ellen
(Netherlands)

Introduction:

When I was invited to write something about China, especially when it was supposed to be about something that captivated me, I soon decided to write about Shanghai. As a professional consulting engineer from the Netherlands in the undertaking of water resource management, I'm fortunate to have traveled to many different cities. But there has never been a place that has given me the same deep impression as Shanghai has. I've lived in Shanghai for six years, but over all the time, this city never fails to impress and surprise

Shanghai—A City of Hope

me. Shanghai is both old and new, fast and slow, and it is a fusion of the East and the West. There is not another place or another city in the world that surpasses Shanghai in this kind of uniqueness and specialness.

June 2004, Shanghai at that time:

The first time that I came to China was in 2004, and most of my time was spent in Shanghai.

During my first weekend in Shanghai, to drink a cup of authentic coffee, I took Line 1 of the subway to the Starbucks in the People's Square. At that time, there were not many places that supplied good, quality coffee. But, before long, I'd found a resolution to my coffee problem, because I found out that I liked Chinese tea very much. I consider tea to be one of the greatest gifts that China has given me.

When speaking of Shanghai, one simply cannot omit the Bund. The Bund, or Waitan, is positioned along the bank of the Huangpu River, and is a coastal pedestrian area 1.5 kilometers in length. The first time that I went to the Bund, a construction colleague of mine brought me. I saw the 468-meter tall Oriental Pearl Radio & TV Tower, and at night it was an exceptionally beautiful sight, connecting Shanghai and the other places of the world together. I also saw the 420-meter tall Jinmao Tower. At the time, I observed enormous cranes, hoisting blocks, and large trucks... and I could foresee that something special was under way.

Later, I took a plane from Hongqiao Airport to Beijing. In my opinion, the only reliable way to get to Hongqiao at the time was taking a taxi. In 2004, Shanghai only had three subway lines, and the running distance was merely 100 kilometers or so. At the time, Hongqiao Airport was only a small-scale,

domestic airport, and was very outdated and overcrowded. The check-in hall was especially small, and the number of people waiting in line was particularly large. I could only hold onto my passport and stand on the sidewalk as I waited to board. Watching the coming and going of the crowded group of people, I estimated that they would need at least an airport twice the size to meet the demand.

But, besides this, what happened on that trip that I will never forget is that I felt the "Shanghai humming" for the first time. It really does exist! Shanghai is full of energy and vitality, which has influenced me, and made me believe that anything and everything can happen. I set my heart on returning to this mystical city one day, to this city full of hope and wishes.

April 2019, Shanghai at the present time:

Well, I made it happen, but it did take me a bit of time. Precisely speaking, it took me about ten years, but I finally returned to Shanghai once again in 2013, right after the Spring Festival. As soon as I stepped off the plane, I again felt the "Shanghai humming" that I spoke of before, and this time its sound was even louder. On the way from Pudong Airport to the hotel, we passed by so many new buildings and bridges; Shanghai had changed so very much. Over the next few days, I went to so many new elegant shopping malls, restaurants, coffee shops, rooftop bars and wine bars that I was almost dazzled. It appeared that Shanghai had kept its promise: to be the only place that could advance so fully and incredibly that people can hardly even believe it.

Now, it is April 2019, and I've lived in Shanghai for six years. During those six years, Shanghai has continued to develop, and has experienced great changes.

Firstly, one no longer needs to take Line 1 to the People's Square if all they want is a cup of coffee. Good coffee can be found on every street corner and in every shopping center. Speaking of the subway, the expansion of its network is almost unbelievable. Now, Shanghai's subway has 16 lines, and approximately 700 kilometers of rail, making it possible to take people to almost any place they want to go in the city. This is the world's largest fast transport system, and currently, it is still continuing its expansion. In a closely compacted cluster of skyscrapers and shopping centers, having quick transport to commute daily in a very busy city has made the construction of Shanghai's subway, to the level it is at today, a very great technological success. If I haven't figured incorrectly, every day they must have laid approximately 100 meters of track, and what's more, it is done in one of the most crowded regions in the world. Just being able to accomplish this part of the project was quite a feat.

Even though cranes and trucks can be found throughout the city, and it seems as though the construction will never come to a halt, Shanghai has gone great lengths to maintain the image of a green and beautiful city. Shanghai has been called the "Magnolia City," and its nickname holds very true to the reality. As a matter of fact, it could also be called the "City of Flowers."

Business

Shanghai has many lovely parks, and each is full of fresh flowers, lawns of green grass, bubbling fountains, and little brooks. Some of the smaller parks are not easy to discover, while other larger parks are very difficult to miss. During all months of the year, flowers are in bloom on the streets, and people water and take care of them almost every day.

The old Hongqiao Airport has long gone. The completely new Shanghai Hongqiao International Airport is modern in style, and is both convenient and fast. Hongqiao International Airport opened international flights to Japan, South Korea, and many other places. The check-in hall is spacious and comfortable, and people no longer need to stand in long lines on the pavement to board their flights. Hongqiao International Airport and Hongqiao Railway Station are also linked; one need only walk 10 minutes from one to the other. Lines 2 and 10 of the subway also go through Hongqiao Airport, providing people with many transport options to and from the airport.

Speaking of public transport, Shanghai has high-speed trains to most cities in China. Every ten to fifteen minutes, a train leaves for Beijing, with the travel time only being four to five hours long. The trains are best known for their punctuality; whereas in Europe, this reliability in timing cannot always be expected.

Another interesting part of Shanghai's public transport, worthy of mention, is the bicycle-sharing system. After registering for the necessary bike-sharing app, every time you go out, you can just scan a bike's QR code and go. After locking it up once you are done, the app automatically charges the small fee to your account; it is incredibly convenient. Presently, Shanghai has the biggest bike-sharing system among all the cities in the world. But what is more important than size, I think, is that it has changed the city's appearance. In the past, Shanghai was full of speeding motorbikes, but now, people prefer

Published by Phoenix Tree Publishing Inc.

Copyright © 2019 Editorial Staff of the book

ALL RIGHTS RESERVED.

No part of this book covered by the copyright hereon may be reproduced or used in any form or by any means—graphic, electronic, including photocopying, taping, web distribution, information storage and retrieval system, or in any other manner, without prior written permission from the publisher.

Phoenix Tree Publishing Inc. has the exclusive right of general distribution of this publication throughout North America (including the United States, Canada and Mexico). No organization or individual is allowed to distribute or sell this publication in North America without prior written permission from Phoenix Tree Publishing Inc. Beijing Language and Culture University Press has the rights of general distribution and sale of this publication in regions outside of North America.

China's Metamorphosis: 35 Global Perspectives
by the Editorial Staff of the book
ISBN: 978-1-62575-265-9
Library of Congress Control Number: 2019946578
First Edition
First Printing: August 2019

Phoenix Tree Publishing Inc.
5660 North Jersey Ave, Chicago, IL 60659
Phone: 773.250.0707   Fax: 773.250.0808
Email: marketing@phoenixtree.com

For information about special discounts for bulk purchases, please contact the publisher at the address above.

Find out more about Phoenix Tree Publishing Inc. at
www.phoenixtree.com

to go to places by bike, making for a livelier city.

Today, the Bund has emerged as an enchanting site for people to visit. At sunset, when the lanterns are lit, the view is especially captivating. Whenever friends or family have come to visit me, the first thing I normally do is take them there. All of them, without exception, marveled at the Bund, and said that it was the most beautiful skyline they'd ever seen. Besides the Oriental Pearl Radio & TV Tower and Jinmao Tower, the Bund now includes the Shanghai World Financial Center (492 meters) and Shanghai Tower (632 meters). Jinmao Tower, the Shanghai World Financial Center, and Shanghai Tower together make up the world's first cluster of three neighboring skyscrapers. Sitting in a rooftop bar, while having a drink, watching the boats glide by below, and gazing at the horizon, is my favorite way to sit back and enjoy an evening.

Lastly, I can't help but say a few words about WeChat—it is the one thing that has had the greatest effect on me since returning to Shanghai. Now, I use WeChat for social media, to make payments, for spending in virtually any place (such as a taxi ride, restaurant, store, or even a small street stand). I only need to provide a WeChat payment QR code, and I can easily make a payment without the use of actual cash or a credit card.

These are only some of the astonishing changes I have seen in Shanghai. Naturally, the future will only bring even more changes. I have no doubt that, in the future, Shanghai will become an even more interesting and happier place to live in. Shanghai welcomes you to come see for yourselves!